When I Grew Up Long Ago

Books on Folklore and Folk Life
by Alvin Schwartz

When I Grew Up Long Ago

FAMILY LIVING, GOING TO SCHOOL,

GAMES AND PARTIES, CURES AND DEATH,

A COMET, A WAR, FALLING IN LOVE,

AND OTHER THINGS I REMEMBER

Older people talk about the days when they were young
collected and
edited by **Alvin Schwartz**

Drawings by Harold Berson

48, 619

J. B. Lippincott Company / Philadelphia and New York

U.S. Library of Congress Cataloging in Publication Data

Schwartz, Alvin, birth date
    When I grew up long ago.

    Bibliography: p.
    Includes index.
    SUMMARY: Brief statements from people whose childhoods were in the period
1890–1914 on such areas of their past lives as food, social life, music, holidays,
and health present glimpses of life in the United States at that time.
    1. United States—Social life and customs—1865–1918—Sources—Juvenile lit-
erature. 2. United States—Social life and customs—20th century—Sources—
Juvenile literature. 3. United States—Biography—Juvenile literature. [1. United
States—Social life and customs—1865–1918—Sources. 2. United States—Social
life and customs—20th century—Sources] I. Berson, Harold. II. Title.
E168.S417   973.8   78–8719
ISBN–0–397–31726–3

Drawings on pages 72, 81, 85, 95–96, and 128
by Barbara Carmer Schwartz

For Gussie Younger Schwartz
and Edna Cox Carmer

Contents

"You forget all this, you forget it all.
I'm so tickled to be talkin' about it. . . ."

A Vanished World

This book is an account of what it was like to be young when the elderly people we know were young. It is drawn from the recollections of men and women in many parts of the country.

The years were roughly 1890 to 1914. It was a seemingly peaceful, uncomplicated time. But it also was a turning point. For in that period this country began to change from a simple rural society to the complex urban society in which we now live.

In 1890 there were about sixty million people in the United States. Two-thirds lived on farms and in small towns. The rest lived in cities. But the pattern of their lives was essentially the same. Unless they were well-to-do, they went to school for only a few years—five years was the average. Then they started work, and eventually they married and raised families. The more adventurous moved west, but the largest number stayed where they were born, near their parents and their other relatives.

They lived seemingly simple lives. In many cases they raised their own food. They also made much of the clothing they wore. When they got sick, they relied on home remedies. Only if an illness became serious did they call a doctor. They found their pleasures with their families and their neighbors. But they seldom "went out" as we do, and they rarely journeyed far from home. Sooner or later they learned about the important events taking place elsewhere, but all that was part of a world beyond their world.

For many years they depended on kerosene lamps, wood stoves and coal stoves, wells, cisterns, and springs, outhouses, and horse-drawn vehicles. Then a remarkable series of advances improved their lives. Soon after the turn of the century they began to acquire telephones, then electric lights, then running water and indoor toilets, then central heating. Many also bought "motorcars." Only ten years after cars first appeared, there were almost half a million in use.

As change quickened, a simple way of life began to disappear. The new technology—the use of telephones, electricity, and cars—was, of course, one reason. But the spread of industry was another. And the growing influence of the United States in the world, and the fearful responsibilities it was assuming, was still another.

By 1914 there were almost a hundred million people in this country. About as many now lived in the cities as on farms and in small towns. The nation was fast becoming an urban place. Most of the people who contributed their memories to this book had finished school and started work. Some already had children of their own. But the world they had known as children no longer existed.

———•———

This book includes several thousand passages taken from one hundred and fifty-six interviews I conducted with older people. A majority of these passages have been edited slightly for clarity or brevity, but they are very close to the informants' exact phrasing. A number include every word the informant used, with any mistakes in phrasing. A few have been retold in my words.

A.S.

My Family

OVER A HUNDRED YEARS AGO

My mother was one of the Indians. When she was very young she was livin' somewhere out from Prescott, and one day there was fightin'. There were lots of soldiers fightin' the Indians, and there was a lot of killin'. Well, Mother was with her sister, and these soldiers were about to get 'em; capture 'em. So her sister run to a jump-off place where even a bird couldn't save his life, and she jumped and killed herself.

All the Indians were killed that day, except for Mother. Then this Army captain found her wandering around, and he made up his mind he was going to take her back to his mother in Skull Valley, and that's what he did. And his mother raised her and taught her to read and write. Then when she got past twelve a woman over in People's Valley asked if she would come and work for her on her ranch. So she did, and she stayed till she was grown.

NEAR PRESCOTT, ARIZONA, ABOUT 1870–1885

My father was born in Grant County, Wisconsin. When he was seventeen he crossed the Plains in a covered wagon with his mother and father and his four brothers and two sisters. They crossed in a wagon train with thirty other families. In one place they were traveling through this stretch of tall grass and suddenly Indian heads were bobbing up all around them. The captain of the train called the wagons to circle, and the men stood guard, and the Indians disappeared. But they traveled all night to get away from them. Then in the morning, farther on down the trail, they came on the ruins of another train. The wagons still were burning, and there were bodies all around. They had several times like that.

GRANT COUNTY, WISCONSIN–LATHROP, CALIFORNIA, 1855

My father was a slave. But when they freed him, he just stayed right where he was. He kept workin' on the same plantation like he did before. Except he wasn't a slave no more.

NEAR ALLISON, SOUTH CAROLINA, ABOUT 1855–1865

Like many former slaves, this man's father became a sharecropper. His former owner rented him a small piece of land, gave him supplies to farm it, and took part of his crop as payment.

My father came from Roscommon, Ireland, when he was seven years old. His folks had died, and he had two sisters in Oshkosh, Wisconsin, and they sent for him. So the neighbors

18

hung a tag around his neck with who he was and where he was going and put him on a boat to Brooklyn, New York. And his sisters met him there and took him home to Oshkosh. He lived with them until he was grown. Then he came to Iowa and farmed.

ROSCOMMON, IRELAND–GREENE, IOWA, 1850–1863

My father's parents came to California from Cincinnati. His father was a cabinetmaker and he took his house apart and brought it with him. They got on a ship someplace and went around Cape Horn to San Francisco. When they got there he unloaded his house and put it up on Kearney Street. That's where my father was born.

My mother's father also came around the Horn. He came to California from Chicago looking for gold. When he got to San Francisco he took a steamboat up the river to Sacramento. And from Sacramento he went by stage to Marysville. Then he went on foot up into the mountains. After a few years he owned several mines and had made quite a lot of money. So he came back to Marysville and settled down and got married. That's where my mother was born.

CINCINNATI–SAN FRANCISCO, ABOUT 1850
CHICAGO–MARYSVILLE, CALIFORNIA, ABOUT 1850–1855

MY MOTHER AND FATHER MEET
AND FALL IN LOVE AND GET MARRIED

My mother was at the theatre with some friends, and on the way home they stopped at this hotel for supper. The man behind the desk was my father. He was a very good-looking young man with golden hair and brown eyes. And she fell for him, and she made it her business to go back for supper again.

BROOKLYN, NEW YORK, ABOUT 1890

My father was walking down this street and saw a couple of girls sitting on a porch poppin' grapes into each other's mouth. One of them caught his eye, and he never rested, he said, until he found somebody to introduce him. Mother said she saw him that day and thought he was cute. But she had never seen him without his hat off until he came to call. Then he turned out to be bald.

NEW ORLEANS, ABOUT 1900

My father was an artist. He had a studio where he gave painting lessons, and Mother was one of his pupils. One day there was a bunch of violets near the door, and as she was leaving he took some of them and pinned them to the lapel of her coat. That was the start of the romance.

STOCKTON, CALIFORNIA, 1897

My father was trying to court my mother's older sister. But he was a bricklayer and she thought he wasn't good enough for her. So he proposed to my mother. She was working in a candy factory and didn't like it. So she was happy to accept his proposal.

INDIANAPOLIS, 1872

Father was a young preacher and had gone up into the mountains to marry somebody. Mother had gone up there as a bridesmaid and she met Father, and he started seeing her. There was a little train he would take and the engineer would stop the train right at the ranch where Mother lived. Then Father would walk across the fields to see her. And so they fell in love and were married.

MARYSVILLE, CALIFORNIA, ABOUT 1880

I AM BORN

*In those days almost everybody was born at home in his parents'
bed. If there was no doctor, usually a relative or a midwife would
help. It was not until after World War I that it became common
to go to a hospital to have a baby.*

My mother had me without any help at all, except that
Grandma cut the cord. She was an expert at that.

CASCADE COUNTY, MONTANA, 1903

Some old lady fetched me out. My mama paid her fifty cents
to do it.

NEAR CADE, LOUISIANA, 1892

A doctor named James Bainbridge delivered me. He lived
eight miles out from us, and my brother went on horseback
to fetch him. Every morning that doctor would get up on his
windmill and look to see if anybody was coming for him. And
that morning he looked and about three miles north he saw
a man on horseback. So he called to his boys to hitch up the
horse so he could be on his way.

NEAR LATHROP, CALIFORNIA, 1888

There was a very fine bachelors' club right next door to our
house. Just about the time I was going to be born they were
having a dinner party, and our doctor was there in his new
dress suit. Before their dinner he and his friends stood at a
window and drank a toast to my parents, who were standing
at a window in our house. When I began to arrive, Father went
over to get him. He delivered me in his new dress suit with
aprons tied over it. I was born in the same bedroom and the
same bed I now use.

TUCSON, ARIZONA, 1901

21

THE FIRST THINGS I REMEMBER

Some of the things I remember are vague. When I think of them it is as if I have been dreaming. But my mother told me I truly was remembering. . . .

DETROIT

My dad was the shoemaker of the town, but he also was some sort of official. His job was to help poor people who needed help. They would come to the house at all hours, even when we were asleep. And Dad would get up and light a lamp and get dressed and talk with them.

MOKRIN, AUSTRIA-HUNGARY, ABOUT 1908

It was a special occasion. I don't remember what, but my mother dressed me up in a pink dress with pink bows on the shoulders, and a white pinafore over the dress, and pink stockings, and pink shoes, and pink hair ribbons, and pink gloves without fingers in them. I felt very grand.

BROOKLYN, NEW YORK, ABOUT 1900

In this park there was a man with a flock of canaries flying around him. When I gave him a coin he told a canary to pick out a fortune for me. So it hopped over to a box where there were a lot of them and it picked one out. Then it flew over and sat on my finger and put the fortune in my hand.

SAN FRANCISCO, ABOUT 1895

We were moving to Nebraska, and I saw a black man for the first time in my life. So I walked up to him and I says, "Hello, Nigger." He was rather shocked, and my mother, she was horrified.

OMAHA, NEBRASKA, ABOUT 1898

I had a sore throat, and Doctor Swift came down from Pleasantville with his horse and buggy to take care of it. We were sitting in the dining room window. He had me on his lap and my shoes and stockings were off because he was patting me on the bottoms of my feet, and he was singing:

"Shoe the old horse, shoe the old mare,
But let the little feet go bare."

HAWTHORNE, NEW YORK, ABOUT 1900

MORE ABOUT MY PARENTS

When I was born my daddy had a little farm. Then he bought a grocery store. Then he sold it and bought a saloon, and he began to drink. Then he went broke. Then he bought a little farm.

NEAR SCOTT, LOUISIANA

After my father made a lot of money in real estate, he took off every summer for three months. All he did was make our kites and help us fly them and run his boats and entertain his friends. We had a very good time.

LOS ANGELES

My stepfather was a gambler. That was his one sport. They had regular gambling places downtown in back of the saloons, and sometimes they'd play cards all night. When he gambled he always had his gun with him. He would wear it in a holster around his waist, but as far as I know he never used it.

MARYSVILLE, MONTANA

My father was a deeply religious person. He believed thoroughly in the Bible, and he expected Jesus Christ to come again a second time. He had no question about it in his mind.

23

Every Sunday he went to church in the morning and again in the evening. And in the afternoon my sister would play the piano for him and he'd sing hymns.

BETHANY, NEBRASKA

My father never joined a church. His father was very strict about religion, and he'd licked him for whistling on Sunday and for cutting kindling for my grandmother and that sort of thing. So my father commenced to wonder, and he decided if that was religion, he didn't want it.

NEAR LATHROP, CALIFORNIA

Mother always slept with a baseball bat right next to her bed in case of burglars.
She didn't count on your father?
She counted on him, but she wasn't going to leave him to deal with this alone. She was such a gentle little lady. You'd never dream what a tiger she could be.

BUCKLEY, ILLINOIS

At the dinner table my father had this awful habit of standing up and reaching for whatever he wanted. And my mother would say, "Someday you're gonna do that, and you're gonna lose a couple of fingers." She'd put up with it just so long. Then she'd bat him one.

CAMBRIDGE, MASSACHUSETTS

When I was twelve or thirteen my mother asked me to keep an eye on my father. She said he had a razor in his pocket and was threatening to kill himself. He was a rich man's son and he had used up all the money he had inherited. Eventually he took to drinking. But he didn't kill himself. I don't think he had the courage.

NEW YORK, UPPER EAST SIDE DISTRICT

My father was fifty-eight when I was born. He had fought at Gettysburg during the Civil War and was twenty-five years older than my mother. He was a lawyer. But he was a very quiet man. I would ride home with him each day after school. And we would ride that whole mile, and he'd never say a word unless I asked him something. But usually I didn't know what to ask.

MARINE CITY, MICHIGAN

My mother and my father never got married. They lived together for a while. Then he went away and she raised us by herself. I don't even remember what he looked like.

NEAR LAFAYETTE, LOUISIANA

After Mama died Poppa done the cookin' until he got tangled up with another one. He was married three times and, the way they tell it, he had twenty-two children. But he never told us he was gettin' married again. Well, after he done it he took his new wife to the house and he says to me, "Here's your new mother." I said, "Okay." But she didn't say too much. She felt a little strange, I guess.

NEW ORLEANS, 1892

After my mother died, my father brought my sister and me to this orphanage. We came right from the train. After that, we saw him just a few more times and that was all. The nuns told us that now we belonged to them.

NEW ORLEANS, 1914

My father was a very tender man. Before he went to sleep each night, he saw that everything was all locked up and that everyone was all covered up. Then he would kiss each of us good night.

WEIMAR, TEXAS

Our House

HOW WE LIVED

The house where I first lived was a little round hut made out of grass. It had a dirt floor and no windows—just an opening to crawl through.

PAPAGO INDIAN VILLAGE NEAR TUCSON, ARIZONA, 1905

Sod houses were common in places where there wasn't wood or stone to build with. The sod was cut from the ground in long strips; then the strips were laid in place like bricks.

When we got off the train in Jerome, my dad rented a house for us. Then he got him a saddle horse and hunted all over the Verde Valley for a suitable ranch. Oh, he hunted all over. Just stayed where night overtook him—slept on his saddle blankets, or a rancher would say, "Come on in."

Well, anyhow, he got us a ranch out there. To begin with we lived in a tent. Then he built a one-room shack and we lived in the tent and the shack. We lived like that four, five years. So for a while things was pretty crude.

The whole tent was maybe fifteen feet by twenty-five feet. And this end was the kitchen, and we had a cookstove here. And that end was the bedroom, and my mother and father slept there.

My brother and I slept out in the yard. We had us a home-made bed made from planks and boards, kind of a big box, and in the bottom there was corn shucks we slept on. And over the top of it we had wagon bows—little strips of wood bent over—and then canvas stretched over that to get the rain off.

The centipedes and scorpions was so thick around there, they'd get inside the tent. So we put boards around at the bottom. Then we put down a board floor. So gradually things got improved.

OAK CREEK, ARIZONA, 1906–1910

Dad had a farm that was all new land. He cut a great big hole in the woods, and he pulled out the stumps and planted potatoes and built us a house. It was just a little house eighteen feet by sixteen feet. There was no shed on it or anything. Downstairs there was the kitchen and a bedroom and upstairs there were two bedrooms. That was all.

MOUNT CHASE, MAINE, 1895

When we came from Italy we lived in this two-room flat on Elizabeth Street. There was a small bedroom where my parents slept and one big room with a kitchen in it. The six children slept there. At night my mother would open up three folding beds for us. Otherwise, there was just a table, a few chairs to sit on, and a kerosene lamp. The toilet was downstairs in the yard. It was a regular outhouse. There were ten of them down there. The water was in the yard, too. You had to pump it, then you'd bring it upstairs in a bucket.

NEW YORK, LOWER EAST SIDE DISTRICT, 1900

Almost a million immigrants from Europe settled in New York's Lower East Side around the turn of the century.

You entered a hallway, and off the hallway was a parlor. In the parlor was a bay window where Mother kept her plants, and there was an organ in that room. Then beyond the parlor was a room that was all done in red. It had a red carpet, red paper on the walls, and a square grand piano.

The other way from the parlor was the dining room, and a buttery where Mother kept her supplies like flour and sugar, and the kitchen. In the kitchen there was a big range with beautiful nickel-plated decorations I would polish just to see them shine. There also was a pump where we would draw soft water from a cistern for the washing of dishes and the washing of clothes. Beyond that was a cellar where they kept the barrels of apples and the barrels of molasses.

Outside the cellar was what we called the buggy shed. That had many parts. It had an icehouse filled with sawdust where they kept the ice they cut in the winter. And it had a place where they kept the corncobs we used to start the fires.

Beyond that was a place where we kept the vehicles—the two-seated carriage and the single-seated buggies and the carts. We would go there and sit for hours and make believe

28

we were driving the team and going on a great journey.

BUCKLEY, ILLINOIS, 1905

We lived in the Bryson Apartments on Wilshire Boulevard. The Bryson was very swanky. A maid would come in every day and do the dishes and clean the apartment. And a man would bring ice for the icebox and take out the garbage. And there was a doorman and an elevator man and somebody to take our telephone calls if we weren't at home.

LOS ANGELES, 1914

It wasn't a big house. It was a medium house. It had a front parlor that was dressed up for visitors, and a back parlor where you sat and read, and a library where all the furniture was red leather, and a music room with a piano and little gold furniture. There also was a large dining room and a big pantry and a big kitchen.

Upstairs we had—let me count—six bedrooms, four for the family and two in back for the maids. And we had two bathrooms for the family and one for the maids. There also was a third floor. We called it the ballroom, but as my brother grew up he used it as a billiard room. Behind the house was a garage with an apartment over it. That was where Mother's chauffeur lived.

DETROIT, 1900

In those days a house with three bathrooms was very unusual. See the sections below on running water and toilets.

CORN SHUCKS AND STRAW

We stuffed corn shucks into a tick and that was our mattress. Then in the spring of the year Mother would wash all the ticks and we'd change the shucks. By then the old shucks was really

29

ground up. But when you got the new ones in, that mattress was about a foot thick and you'd sink right into it. Oh, it was soft, we thought.

OSAGE COUNTY, MISSOURI, 1890

A tick is a cloth bag used for mattresses and pillows. Besides corn shucks, farm families stuffed their mattresses with straw, Spanish moss, duck feathers, or goose feathers. Of course, most city families had to buy their mattresses.

RUNNING WATER

I sat at the kitchen sink and Grandma would pump water on a comb and make water curls. She'd clack her false teeth and pump on the pump and make two rows all around my head. Then she'd tie a bow in place.

HAWTHORNE, NEW YORK, 1905

The pump usually was in the kitchen or just outside. So it was there that people washed and brushed their teeth and combed their hair. Or they kept water pitchers and washbasins in their rooms and took care of these things there.

At least once a week, almost everybody took a bath. Usually bathing also was done in the kitchen. The bathtub was a washtub filled with hot water from the stove. If you were small enough, you could sit down by drawing your knees to your chest. Otherwise, you washed yourself standing up. Often all the women and girls in the family bathed together. Then the men and boys did. In most families people bathed on Saturday night because on Sundays they went to church.

A smaller number of families had running water in their homes. But they could only have running water if there was a water system where they lived and if they could afford the plumbing.

Some people had bathtubs in their homes as early as 1895, but many others did not have their first bath in a bathtub until 1910 or later, when they were fifteen or sixteen years old.

TOILETS

Our outhouse was just a little shed about thirty, forty feet back. To keep it hidden, we had a trellis in front with a grape-vine growing on it, and also some rosebushes. There were three holes, a little one for children and two big-size holes. That was so two or three of us could use it at the same time, if we were the same sex. You always went out there just before you went to bed. You had a lantern with you, but it was spooky and in the winter it was cold. If you had to go during the night there was a chamber pot under every bed. In the morning we emptied them into a big white slop pot, then dumped the slop pot into the outhouse.

HAWTHORNE, NEW YORK, 1905

This woman's uncle was the richest man in town, and he had a flush toilet in his house. It had a water tank above the bowl and a chain you pulled to make it flush. He also had regular toilet paper there. It came in sheets that hung on a hook. Of course, many people still were using newspaper for toilet paper, or pages from mail-order catalogs or telephone books, or the orange tissue paper used to keep oranges from being bruised.

HEAT

There was a stove downstairs, but there wasn't one upstairs. So in the winter we'd undress by that stove. Then we'd run upstairs and jump into bed. If it was really cold, Mother would heat up a log in the oven, get it nice and warm, and put it in

31

bed with us. In the morning we'd jump out of bed and skiddoo
—get right back to that stove and get dressed there.

MOUNT CHASE, MAINE, 1895

*"Skiddoo" means "get moving" or "get out." It is related to
"skedaddle."*

*Almost everybody depended on wood stoves or coal stoves to keep
warm. In some houses there was only one. In others there was one
in every room. Once or twice a day somebody had to bring in more
wood or more coal, and somebody had to haul out the ashes. Then
at night the fires would be banked, and in the morning someone
would get up early and get them going again. In the 1890s coal
furnaces and steam radiators were being installed here and there,
but it was quite a while before most people had them.*

LIGHT

*Many families used oil lamps that burned kerosene, or "coal oil,"
as it also was called. They were inexpensive, but they were a lot
of trouble. Every day or so you had to take up the glass chimneys
and clean the soot from them, and trim the wicks so the lamps
would burn properly, and add more kerosene.*

*Some families had gas lights. These were attached to gas jets
in the ceilings and walls and burned illuminating gas, which was
piped in. Each light had a mantle that was ignited with a match.
By the turn of the century, there were homes with electric lights.*

The first night we had electricity, Mother turned on all the
lights in every room. Then we went outside and walked up the
street to the corner and walked slowly back, and she said, "I
never thought that this house would look like that." It was just
a blaze of light.

INDEPENDENCE, MISSOURI, 1905

Electric light was *brighter and steadier than gaslight. But to many people what was really remarkable was that all you did was turn a switch and the light came on.*

TELEPHONES

When we got our telephone, that was quite a thing. If you needed to find out something, you didn't have to go on foot or hitch up a buggy or write a letter. You just used the telephone. It was a big wooden box stuck up on the wall, so you had to stand up to talk. You couldn't sit down. There was a mouthpiece that came out of the center, and a receiver that came out of the side. When you picked up the receiver, the operator asked for the number you wanted, and she rang it for you. Actually you could hear pretty well. But whenever we used the phone, we tended to raise our voices. It seemed such a distance when you talked to somebody four, five blocks away.

INDIANAPOLIS, 1905

What We Ate

Around the turn of the century, breakfast was breakfast. But while we usually have lunch at noon and dinner in the evening, most people ate dinner in the middle of the day and supper, a very light meal, at night. Lunch was the name for a late evening snack.

WHERE WE GOT OUR FOOD

We bought our supplies in Cascade. That was about eighteen miles over the mountain from our place. Twice a year we'd take the wagon and four horses and go down there and buy five hundred pounds of flour, five hundred pounds of sugar,

34

four, five slabs of bacon, hams, molasses, corn syrup, coffee, stuff like that, enough to last half a year. Then we'd take a few hours to look around, and head back. But comin' out, climbin' back into the mountains, it was all a slow luggin'. Often we wouldn't get home till after dark.

CASCADE COUNTY, MONTANA, 1910

Each morning Mother would tell the cook what she wanted for dinner, and the cook would make up a grocery list. Then at a regular time the man from the grocery store would come over on his bicycle and get the order and bring back what we needed.

TUCSON, ARIZONA, 1910

My mother did her shopping in a store on the corner. She had a little brown book the grocer gave us, and he'd write in that book what we took and what it cost. Then about twice a month we'd pay him. Everybody did that. When we paid, he'd give us a bag about that high with candy and, oh, just little things he felt perhaps we needed. It was sort of a gift for trading there.

SEATTLE, 1910

In that store there was a counter where the people were served, and there were shelves all around where canned goods were kept. And there was this great round coffee grinder with a big wheel on it, and they'd turn the wheel and grind the coffee fresh. And there was flour and sugar and molasses in barrels, and cheese and butter in tubs, and toward the back these big tins of kerosene. In the middle of the store there was a big heating stove. Then on the other side was the post office, and next to it was where they kept the candy.

HAWTHORNE, NEW YORK, 1905

A grocery wagon would come to the house maybe once, twice a week. He'd have all the standard things already weighed out in paper bags, like sugar, flour, coffee, hardtack, and he'd have some canned goods and so forth. If you wanted molasses you handed him your jug, and the next time he'd bring it back filled. If there was something else you wanted, he'd write it down and bring that back, too.

There also was a meat wagon that came around. It was just a big horse-drawn wagon with a wooden roof on the back. It looked like a big box. The butcher, he had a butcher block back there and his tools and a hanging scales with a hook on it. You'd look inside and tell him what you wanted, and he'd cut it off and put it on the hook and weigh it.

MARTHA'S VINEYARD, MASSACHUSETTS, 1910

Early in the morning the fish vendors would go down to the Columbus Street wharf to meet the fishing boats when they came in. If they had shrimp, they'd fill these great huge platters and balance them on their heads and walk along as gracefully as you ever saw. And up on top the shrimp would be jumpin' and kickin'. They'd come along callin', "Shrimpee! Shrimpeeee! Shrimpeee-eee!" If they also had fish or oysters they'd bring them in a bucket.

CHARLESTON, SOUTH CAROLINA, 1905

The milkman came in a horse cart and his milk was in five-gallon cans. He had a quart measure, and we had a container of some kind, usually an old lard can, and he'd just dip out what we needed.

TUCSON, ARIZONA, 1910

Mostly we ate out of the farm. We had hogs and we slaughtered them, and we had cows and used the milk, and now and then Father would butcher a calf. And we had chickens. And

36

Mother'd put up tomatoes and dried apples and make sauerkraut. Just slice up some cabbage, put a little salt on it, put it in big stone jars, and let it ferment. She fixed turnips that way, and beans and beets. Then twice a week she'd bake bread, and when she had fruit, we'd get a pie. We ate very simple.

OSAGE COUNTY, MISSOURI, 1890

Almost every farmer raised at least a few hogs for meat. Some people in small towns also did. Fattening a hog in the spring and the summer and slaughtering it in the fall was an American ritual.

First off, we'd kill him with a rifle. We'd shoot him just above one of his eyes. When he dropped, we'd stick him in the throat and bleed him. Then after the blood stopped, we'd scald him. That would loosen the hair on his body so we could scrape it off.

We had a big pot three, four feet across that was bricked up all around, and we'd fill that with water and get a fire goin' underneath. When the water got just hot enough, almost boilin' but not quite, we'd pick up the hog and put him in the pot for a minute or two. Then we'd take him out, and Pop would scrape him up and down with this scraper and get all the hair off.

When he was finished, we would tie the hind legs together and hang that hog from a cross pole, then wash him down with a hose. Oh, he would look just as clean and white. Then we'd cut off his head and cut him into pieces.

NEAR STOCKTON, CALIFORNIA, 1910

When they "stuck" a hog in the throat, they tried to pierce its jugular vein. It is on the left side about three inches behind the jawbone.

37

Some Indian tribes still depended for their food on wild plants and game.

To get along we would gather wild plants in the desert, and the men would go out each day with bows and arrows and kill animals for meat—rabbits, muskrats, little wild pigs, deer, things like that. When it rained enough to fill the *arroyos* [dry streambeds], they would go there early in the morning and kill the animals that came to drink. Then sometimes a cow would come in from some other place without a brand on it. So they would kill it and divide the meat and jerk it.

PAPAGO INDIAN VILLAGE NEAR TUCSON, ARIZONA, 1905

"Jerking" meat was one way of preserving it. The meat was cut into strips and dried in the sun, which produced what is called "jerky." There were many other methods of preserving food that country people used. When a farmer slaughtered a hog, for example, the meat was kept in jars of brine, or it was fried and stored in its grease, or it was smoked in a smokehouse and stored there. Vegetables, milk, and butter might be kept in a cool basement, or in a "cave"—a hole dug in the ground with a cover on it—or in a screened box in a stream. In the north, farmers cut ice from ponds and stored some of their food in iceboxes. City people also used iceboxes, but they depended on ice men who came each day to deliver the ice they needed.

PREPARING MEALS

When you ask what it was like to do the cooking in those days, one of the first things you are told is how much time it took. Often a woman and her daughter, or a servant, spent half a day or more getting meals.

It wasn't that the meals were complicated. There was less variety and more plain cooking than there is today. But every dish had to be prepared from its basic ingredients.

In addition, the equipment was difficult to use. A few families had gas ranges with adjustable burners, but most depended on ranges that used wood or coal, and with these there was no way to adjust the heat except by adjusting the fire underneath. And when you did that, all the pots were affected. Also, an oven did not have a temperature gauge, so a cook had to keep a close eye on things.

But one Iowa woman said, "The meals were just as good then, and sometimes they were better." A lot of people agreed.

EATING TOGETHER

The elder people would sit on benches at the table. The children would sit on the floor. They'd give you a little tin pan of food and a spoon to eat it with and tell you to don't spill none. And you were just so glad to get it.

Why did you use just a spoon?

Because that's all we had. That's all they gave us. The man [who owned this plantation] would come around and sell us these tin pans and these spoons. But no forks, no knives, no nothin'. So you just spooned it out.

NEAR ABBEVILLE, LOUISIANA, 1905

These families were sharecroppers.

We ate our dinner at the dining room table. Daddy always wore a coat and a tie, and we had to be neat and tidy and have our hair brushed. And Mother would serve the vegetables and he would carve the meat.

LOS ANGELES, 1914

We had an old mammy cook who wore a bandana around her head, and she prepared the meals. And we had a very trim, neat-lookin' maid named Virginia, and she waited on table and washed the dishes. All we had to do was eat.

DETROIT, 1905

We did not eat together. Just when we felt like it we would eat. That was the custom. There was always some kind of a tortilla, or they made up some kind of meat or other things. When I was hungry I would go ahead and fill a bowl and sit out in the *ramada* and eat. Then I would clean it and put it away.

PAPAGO INDIAN VILLAGE NEAR TUCSON, ARIZONA, 1905

A ramada *was a community building with a roof supported by posts but no walls.*

ASKING THE BLESSING

Before a meal it was the custom in many families to give thanks to God for their food. They called it "asking the blessing."

Thank you, Lord, for what we are having today.

TUCSON, ARIZONA, 1910

Thank you for the sunshine and the rain and for this food and for the hands that prepared it.

FRANKLIN COUNTY, GEORGIA, 1895

We thank Thee for the food we are about to eat. We ask that You bless it so that it may strengthen our bodies and help us to do the right thing.

MORMON SETTLEMENT, BEAR RIVER CITY, UTAH, 1900

Thank you, God, for providing for us today. Bless us because we are together. Bless us as we go our separate ways.

NEW ORLEANS, 1910

Did your father or mother ever ask a blessing?
Only when the preacher come.

LYNCHBURG, VIRGINIA

BREAKFAST, DINNER, SUPPER

We had a patch of watermelon nearby. So early in the morning when it was cool and fresh we'd sit on the back steps and eat melon. Then we would go to the fields.

NEAR CADE, LOUISIANA, 1900

For breakfast we would have a piece of bread and a cup of black coffee, and that was all.

NEW YORK, LOWER EAST SIDE DISTRICT, 1905

There would be oatmeal and pancakes and beefsteak or ham and pie and coffee and milk. The hired hands ate with us, so altogether there would be about twelve at the table.

BUCKLEY, ILLINOIS, 1905

Every morning we would have half of an orange, and a bowl of oatmeal, and a cup of cocoa.

BROOKLYN, NEW YORK, 1900

You could buy oranges in larger cities, but they were expensive. Elsewhere you only could get them at Christmas, and then they were used as gifts and decorations. But oatmeal was practically a national cereal. In those days it was cooked for several hours the night before. Then it was warmed up the next morning, and

41

you ate it with cream and sugar, or with maple syrup or cane sugar
syrup. The only packaged dry cereal at that time was Grape-Nuts.

At dinnertime my mother would say, "Everything is ready now. Come to the table." So we would do that. Then we would hesitate a little and she would say, *"Yak lai."* That means "Start in to eat." Always we would have a common bowl of soup. Each of us was given a spoon, and the bowl was passed around from one person to the next, and we would eat from it. Then we would have rice and salted meat, or Chinese sausages maybe, and different vegetables.

SAN FRANCISCO, CHINESE DISTRICT, 1905

Sundays there would be chicken on top of chicken. And there'd be corn on the cob and creamed corn and corn pudding. And there'd be mashed potatoes and vegetables. And there'd be three kinds of bread—biscuits, rolls, and corn bread or light bread. And there'd be ice cream and cake. Enough to make you bust.

ROCKBRIDGE COUNTY, VIRGINIA, 1910

We would start with a soup or a shrimp cocktail or a crabmeat cocktail. Then for the second course we would have potatoes or rice or grits. Then we would have chicken, meat, or fish and a vegetable. Then there would be a salad. During the meal the grown-ups would have wine, and I would get one glass. Then there would be dessert and coffee.

NEW ORLEANS, 1905

For dinner we would have some kind of a sandwich, or we would have soup. My mother would make chicken soup with noodles or beef soup with potatoes. But before we could eat it she would take out the meat and save it for Sunday. Then we would have coffee, but no dessert. Dessert was for special occasions.

HAMTRAMCK, MICHIGAN, 1914

Dessert usually was pie, cake, cookies, pudding, or ice cream, just as it is today. Of course, in those days all desserts were homemade. But making ice cream meant cranking a freezer for an hour or more, and in some places ice wasn't always available. So ice cream wasn't served very often. A woman in Utah told me about an old man she knew when she was young who had never tasted ice cream. So she and her friends brought him some, and he took a taste and said he guessed he'd have to warm it up.

Supper for many people was jam and bread, or bananas and bread, or biscuits with sugar cane syrup, or cornmeal mixed with a little water, then cooked in a little grease (people in western Louisiana called this couscous*), or sauerkraut, or cold meat, or whatever was left over from dinner.*

WASHING DISHES

We'd heat some water on the stove and use one dishpan to wash and another to rinse. Then we'd wipe it all and put it away. Some meals it would take an hour or more.

GREENE, IOWA, 1900

RECIPES FOR CANDY AND DESSERTS

Some people I visited still make the same candy and the same desserts they ate when they were young. "Have you ever tried this?" they would ask me. "It is so good."

43

WALNUT CANDY

When my grandfather moved to his plantation right after the Civil War he planted black walnut trees on both sides of a road a mile long. By the time I was a boy those trees were grown, and we would go down there each fall and gather a wagonload of nuts. Then we'd crack 'em open and make walnut candy.

First we'd put brown sugar in a pan with a little water and heat it. When the sugar got melted we'd pile in the walnuts and stir 'em all around. Oh, it was good eatin'.

DAYTON COUNTY, GEORGIA, 1900

BROWN SUGAR PIE

You need a pound of sugar, three eggs, and a piece of butter big as a hen egg. Then you beat all that up and bake it in a pie shell until it's ready.

FINCASTLE, VIRGINIA, 1910

Bake this at about 350 degrees for thirty to forty minutes, or until the filling is firm.

SEMILUNAR PIES

Mother'd stew some apples or peaches and sweeten them and work them up into a mulch. Then she'd roll out some pie dough and put some fruit on top and fold the dough over so the round edges met. When they were ready she'd put them in a skillet with grease and fry them and turn them and fry them some more. And they were just as crisp and good. When we took Latin we called them "semilunar pies." That's the way they looked, like half moons.

BEDFORD COUNTY, TENNESSEE, 1895

These also were called fried pies.

44

OATMEAL COOKIES

This is the way the old recipe card read:

1 cup of flour	2 eggs
2 scant cups of brown sugar	salt
3 cups of rolled oats	4 tablespoons of sweet milk
1 cup of lard and butter mixed	1 small teaspoon of soda
	a half a cup of walnut meats
1 teaspoon of cinnamon	a half a cup of raisins
1 teaspoon of nutmeg	

The lard and butter and sugar should be creamed together, then the eggs put in, then the rest. Mix thoroughly.

DETROIT, 1900

Instead of mixing lard and butter, you can use just butter or margarine. "Sweet milk" is the same as regular milk. A half teaspoon of salt is enough. Bake the cookies at 350 degrees for six or seven minutes or until they are lightly browned around the edges. This recipe will give you about a hundred cookies.

RØD GRØD

When we had canned fruit my mother would take the juice and stir in potato flour or cornstarch until it thickened into a fruit-juice pudding. Then we'd eat it with cream poured on.

LARAMIE, WYOMING, 1910

This is a Danish dessert. It is pronounced "rohd grohd." Stir in about a tablespoon of cornstarch for every cup of fruit juice. Then heat and stir until the mixture is clear and thick. Then cool. If you eat it with cream it becomes "rohd grohd mid flohde." Say that three times fast.

45

What We Wore

HOW BOYS DRESSED

Until I was five or six I wore dresses. All little boys did. Usually it was a red dress so my mother could find me when I got out in the fields.

NEAR FINCASTLE, VIRGINIA, 1898

The boys in our tribe wore just a belt around their waists. And they'd hang a piece of cloth over the belt in front and a piece of cloth behind. Then they slipped a piece of string between their legs and tied the front piece and the back piece together. The older boys wore little pants underneath, but not the younger ones.

PAPAGO INDIAN VILLAGE NEAR TUCSON, ARIZONA, 1910

The only clothes I had were these two shirts that came down to my knees. My mother made 'em from flour sacks. They had printin' all over 'em, but when you washed 'em and ironed 'em they looked purty good. Sort of white. I was ten, eleven before I got any pants.

NEAR ALLISON, SOUTH CAROLINA, 1890

Among black sharecroppers in the South, it was common at that time for young boys to dress this way. Many groups used the cloth from flour sacks for underwear, bathing suits, dish towels, napkins, and a lot of other things. This was so until the 1950s, when paper sacks replaced the cloth ones.

Our shirts weren't too different than they are now, except that they were called "bodies" and "shirtwaists." When you were young you buttoned them to your pants all the way around.

BUENA VISTA, VIRGINIA, 1905

The first pants I wore were straight pants that came down to my knees. Then when I was seven or eight I started wearing knickers with long stockings, and also overalls. It wasn't until I was sixteen or so that I got long pants. The first day you wore them, the other kids would corner you and take 'em away. You'd get them back after a while, but it made you kind of nervous.

TUCSON, ARIZONA, 1910

When it was cold I wore long woolen underwear, all one piece. It came down to my ankles and my wrists and buttoned

47

up the front and unbuttoned at the seat. Then when it got warm I wore cotton underwear. It had a top with short sleeves and a bottom that came down to my knees. Of course, everybody slept in their underwear, and you only changed it when you needed to. That was two, three times a week.

LYNCHBURG, VIRGINIA, 1905

At first I wore button shoes, the kind that buttoned up the front. Then I wore bulldog shoes. These had shoelaces and a big square front on them. The first thing you did when you got shoes like that was to step on them good and hard and break down that front. If you didn't, somebody else would and your foot would be inside. Of course, in the summertime I went barefooted. That first day when I got those shoes off it always seemed like I could fly.

JACKSON COUNTY, MISSOURI, 1910

HOW GIRLS DRESSED

I would wear these great wide muslin dresses that hung down to my ankles. I had one to wear and one to wash. But they were both the same. The Pima Indians made the muslin, and we traded our pottery for it. Then my grandmother made the dresses.

PAPAGO INDIAN VILLAGE NEAR TUCSON, ARIZONA, 1905

When I worked in the field I wore a dress and a slip and underwear, and I went barefooted. The dress came up to my neck and down to my knees and gathered around my waist, and it had long sleeves. And to keep the sun off, I wore a sailor hat with a broad brim.

BANKS COUNTY, GEORGIA, 1895

Around the turn of the century grown women wore their dresses down to their ankles. But if you were fourteen or fifteen or younger, you wore yours down to your knees—and no further. In Uvalde, Texas, and in other places girls were "just dying" to wear them longer, but their mothers wouldn't let them. "They didn't think it proper."

We went to school in middy blouses like the ones the sailors wore, with great big square collars and white braid and a couple of stars in the corners. If you could get hold of a real sailor's tie to go with that middy blouse, that was really something. We wore these blouses with pleated skirts, either navy blue or white. Of course, *the* way to wear them was real tight over your hips. So we'd take them in with safety pins.

LOS ANGELES, 1912

For each outfit you had to have a matching hair ribbon. You just bought it by the yard and tied it, but they were tremendous things. It was a wonder we didn't all blow away.

TACONY, PENNSYLVANIA, 1910

First I'd put on an undershirt that came to about my hips. Then I'd put on a pantywaist over that. Then I pulled on my drawers and buttoned them to the waist. Then I pulled on my stockings and fastened *them* to the waist. After that I put on my bloomers and my petticoat and my dress or whatever. When I started to get a bosom, I started with the undershirt. Then I wore a corset cover that was shaped to fit my figure. Then I put on the rest of it.

HAWTHORNE, NEW YORK, 1905–1910

For everyday I wore black ribbed stockings and plain low shoes, brown or yellow. But one year everybody was wearing gaily colored stockings so I got a pair of blue ones with little

49

white dots. Of course, when I went to parties I wore silk stockings and patent leather sandals.

BROOKLYN, NEW YORK, 1910

When I was seventeen I bought a piece of gingham and made a dress out of it. Well, I had some of that material left over, so I took it and covered my shoes with it by driving pins into the soles. When I went to church that Sunday their eyes like to have bulged out of their heads.

"Look at Ada!" they said. "Her dress and her shoes are made of the same material!"

Well, there I was just bustin' out all over. They had never seen anything like it, and neither had I.

HAMPTON COUNTY, SOUTH CAROLINA, 1906

WHERE WE GOT OUR CLOTHES

My mother made our dresses and our underwear, and she made the boys' shirts and pants, and she made my daddy's shirts and things for herself. She'd use cloth she'd spin on the wheel and cloth from flour sacks and sugar sacks. And she'd knit our stockin's. But we bought our shoes and my daddy bought his overalls.

CARROLL COUNTY, GEORGIA, 1905

Susan Suggins made our clothes. She was a dressmaker, and she would come and live in for the time it took to make them. She would be here in the spring for two or three weeks and then again in the fall. Of course, whenever she was here she ate with us and was one of the family.

Before she came we talked about what we would like to have, and Mother would get samples of fabric and various patterns, and we would decide. Then Susan Suggins would arrive, and she would go up into the ballroom. There was an old square piano up there we used for our parties, and she would use the top of that to cut out the patterns on. Then she had our sewing machine and a big table to work on. She would be up there day after day cutting and pinning and stitching until finally she finished.

HELENA, MONTANA, 1905

Mother bought most of our clothes at Lord & Taylor's and at Macy's and at places like that. But when we needed suits and other special things, they were made by this tailor. We would go to him and stand there and be fitted.

NEW YORK, UPPER EAST SIDE DISTRICT, 1900

WASHING AND IRONING

We'd soak those clothes in a tub full of hot soapy water, then battle 'em [beat them] with a battlin' stick, then rub 'em up and down on a rub board. That was to get the dirt loose. Then we'd put 'em in a big old iron pot and boil the hound out of 'em, then wring 'em through two or three washes and hang 'em up. The next day we'd iron 'em. Every week we'd do that.

CARROLL COUNTY, GEORGIA, 1905

A rub board is a washboard. A battling stick is a small paddle three or four inches across at the bottom. Usually somebody in a family would whittle it out of a piece of board.

The laundry soap this family used was homemade. They filled an ash hopper with wood ashes from their stove. Then they poured water through the hopper and caught the drippings at the bottom. As the water dripped through, it turned to lye, which is a harsh cleaning agent. Then they cooked the lye with the grease from bacon rinds, ham skins, and other fat. As it cooled, it turned into a very strong soap. People had been making soap this way for thousands of years.

51

At that time you could buy a washing machine for three or four dollars. But all it did was help loosen the dirt. Instead of battling and rubbing, you worked a crank back and forth. But before that you still had to soak the clothes, and afterwards you still had to boil them and rinse them two or three times.

To do the ironing, you used flatirons. These looked something like today's irons, but they were solid metal and came in various shapes and sizes. You'd heat several on your stove, use one until it cooled, then put it back and use another.

Of course, some families had servants who did all this, and others had a washwoman who came in for about a dollar a day. But a great many did all their washing and ironing themselves.

Peddlers

Some peddlers came in a wagon with a horse. And some came on the train or the stage. And some walked with a pack on their back. And some was sellin' needles and pins. And some was sellin' other things like soup stones.

"Yes, ma'am," they would say. "You just put this little stone in a pot and add water and cook it awhile and it'll give you a pretty good soup. Then add some leftovers and other stuff and cook it up some more, and it'll give you an even better soup." Of course, they sold quite a few.

OAK CREEK, ARIZONA, 1910

One hears this story in so many places that peddlers probably did sell a soup stone now and then. But mostly they sold what people needed. Some of it was food, but there were many other things as well. A man from Bristol, Tennessee, told me, "If you waited long enough you could get almost anything you needed through a peddler—that and the Sears, Roebuck catalog."

There was this man who drove a covered wagon over from New York. Once or twice a year he would come, and he would stop at every house. He had just about everything in that wagon—pots, pans, knives, pretty dishes, yard goods, ribbons, buttons, sewing things, shawls, handkerchiefs, even whiskey, I heard it said.

MARTHA'S VINEYARD, MASSACHUSETTS, 1895

Every day peddlers would come into the apartment house where we lived, dragging a great big suitcase with them. They'd open it right there in the hallway, and there might be pots in it, or a sewing machine or jewelry or almost anything. If you wanted something and you couldn't pay the whole price, they'd trust you. Every week they'd come back and you'd give them twenty-five cents until it was paid off. That was how we got our petticoats.

NEW YORK, LOWER EAST SIDE DISTRICT, 1900

In many cities there also was a man who would sharpen your scissors and knives right out in the street. He'd have a cart he pushed, and he'd ring a bell and call, "Scissors to sharpen! Scissors to sharpen!" Then people would bring him their things, and he'd sit at one end of his cart and make his grindstone go around and sharpen them up.

And if you needed your chimney cleaned, there were men or boys who would do that. A woman in New Orleans told me about a man who wore a high silk hat and a long-tailed coat and carried

54

a bushy-looking broom made out of dried palmetto leaves. For a nickel he'd scramble up on top of a house, stick his broom in the chimney, swish it up and down, and knock the soot into the fireplace. Then he'd gather it up and carry it off.

Out in the country, peddlers also brought the news. "They would pull into the yard," one woman remembered, "and tell all the happenings up and down: babies born, people married, people died. And we would tell what we knew. Then they carried our news on to the others."

If a peddler arrived toward dark, he might spend the night.

There was this one peddler we would see three, four times a year. He walked with a pack on his back, and he always made it to our house the last thing. And we'd get him up a good supper and he'd stay till morning.

Then after he ate he'd show us all his things. Oh, he'd have just everything in that pack—suspenders and ties and combs and shirts and underwear and knives and razors and jewelry. And he'd spread them all out on the floor, and we'd sit and look at them, and my father would buy whatever he needed.

Then afterwards they would sit and talk about the weather and politics and the place where he grew up across the sea and places he had been and what they were like. Then in the morning after breakfast he would go on his way.

FRANKLIN COUNTY, GEORGIA, 1895

How We Got Around

Sometimes we used a horse and wagon or a horse and buggy. But ten or twelve miles was as far as you ever drove, and that took maybe two hours. Mostly we just walked. When I went to town I'd walk in and walk back. That was eight miles, but I never thought anything of it.

NEAR SHANNON CITY, IOWA, 1905

If we wanted to go someplace, we'd take a streetcar or the "el," or if it was a special occasion we'd engage a horse and carriage.

BROOKLYN, NEW YORK, 1905

The first streetcars were pulled by mules or horses, but by the turn of the century many were running on electricity, and people began calling them "trolley cars" for the wheel, or trolley, that drew the electricity from a wire. "El" was short for "elevated." This was a train with a few cars and a little steam engine that ran on a structure above the street. Some cities still have them, but, of course, the steam engines are gone.

My grandparents had a farm near St. Louis, and every summer we used to go down there on the train. It would be so hot they'd keep the windows open, but there weren't any screens, so the cinders and the soot from the engine would fly in and get all over you, sometimes stick in your eye. Then every hour or so a boy ran through the cars selling bananas and popcorn and everything. But we'd always take a lunch.

INDEPENDENCE, MISSOURI–HANNIBAL, MISSOURI, 1905

I was in the third grade, and it was in the spring and the windows in the schoolhouse were wide open. And all at once we felt this thumping and heard this sound. Eldon Levitt, he reached up like a crane and listened. Then he said, "Good hell! Look a-comin'!" It was a car, the first one we'd ever seen. He jumped up and jumped out the window and chased it. Then so did the rest of us.

BUNKERVILLE, NEVADA, 1907

In 1900 there were about eight thousand automobiles in the country. In 1910 there were almost a half million. The roads they used were dirt, or they were paved with planks, cobblestones, brick, wood blocks set in tar, macadam, or asphalt. If there were street-lights, usually they were gas, and each night they were turned on one by one. In Tucson, Arizona, a man on horseback did this, reaching up from his saddle to ignite the gas. Some larger cities were install-ing electric streetlights. Instead of light bulbs, these used carbon rods that sputtered and hissed from towers high above the street.

What School Was Like

School took up at nine. Then there was recess at ten-thirty and lunch at noon and school again at one and out at three. We started in September, finished in May.

NEAR SHANNON CITY, IOWA, 1900

I'd get up and get the cows in and milk them and get the horses and the hogs fed. Then we'd get ourselves fed. Then

I'd stick my books and my lunch in a pail and go to school. Across the fields it was two miles, and I'd run all the way.

I lived up the creek seven miles, so I rode a horse to school. Everybody did. We'd tie them to the bushes outside and throw our saddles under the schoolhouse.

I went to school on a streetcar and came home that way. But I had to be home on time, right on the minute, or I was in trouble. This was a big dangerous city. That's what my mother thought.

OUR SCHOOLHOUSE

At first there was no school. Then when I was thirteen they had enough kids, and they built one in Trout Creek and got a teacher. Then after one season he left and they couldn't get another one. So I never went to school no more.

We had a high school, but we didn't have a building. We held our classes in people's houses, so we had to move around quite a bit. The upstairs room in our house was where we learned to sew. We had our English class in a woodshed with a tin roof and chicken-wire walls. We had two benches in there and a chair for the teacher. The trees all around were full of aphids of some kind, which meant that there were lizards, which meant that there were doodlebugs, which meant that there were all kinds of things to see.

It was just a common one-room school. There was a big coal stove in the center and desks on both sides. At the front the teacher had a big chair and a table set up on a platform six, eight inches off the floor. Then in front of the platform there was a recitation bench where each grade came to recite. Then behind her was the blackboard. By the time you got there in the morning, she already had built a fire and done the janitor work. Then she taught every grade from one to twelve.

NEAR GREENE, IOWA, 1890

Over behind this hill there was an outhouse for the boys and over beyond that one was an outhouse for the girls. When you raised your hand to leave, you'd put up one finger or two fingers so the teacher would know how long you might be gone.

EDGEWOOD, TEXAS, 1914

There wasn't any drinking water, so usually two kids went after it. You'd go to the nearest house with a bucket. It was quite a thing to do that. It was during classes, you see, and you got out of class. But you had to be good or she wouldn't send you. Then everybody who wanted a drink would line up and use the same bucket and the same dipper. We didn't know too much about germs.

NEAR SHANNON CITY, IOWA, 1900

Because we were colored there was a separate school for us. There was one room downstairs and one room upstairs. But the seventh grade was as far as you could go. The white people had a high school, but we didn't have any. To go to high school, you had to move away.

FINCASTLE, VIRGINIA, 1910

I went to P.S. [Public School] 6. That was at 85th Street and Madison Avenue. There were fifty pupils in every class, and there were four floors of classes. And at every landing there were monitors so you wouldn't talk. Then the gym was on the fifth floor and the toilets were in the basement. There was this long row of seats down there with tiny partitions between them, but no doors, and underneath the seats there was this trough with water running through it.

NEW YORK, UPPER EAST SIDE DISTRICT, 1900

Our school was a two-story brick building with a high board fence all the way around. And there were two yards with a fence between—one for girls, one for boys. On top of the building there was a bell, and at half-past eight they'd ring it good and loud, and when you heard it you started to school. At nine o'clock they'd ring it again, and the girls got into one line and the boys got into another and you marched into your room.

TUCSON, ARIZONA, 1895

WHAT WE LEARNED

Some teachers had a year of teachers' college or what then was called normal school. But many began teaching when they finished high school and weren't much more than eighteen. Almost all the teachers were women. If they didn't live at home, usually they boarded with one of the local families. If they got married, they couldn't teach anymore—that was the rule almost everywhere.

When I first started, we had chart classes. They were a little like kindergarten. The teacher had these big charts she would put on an easel. Each one had a picture and a sentence that described it, and we'd talk about it.

61

There was one that showed this woodsman's house in Maine, and there was this great moon and these evergreen trees and a moose walking in front. And I thought if I ever got to Maine I would see something like that.

She also would write in chalk on our desks. She'd write CAT, DOG, and other words in big letters. Then we'd take these dried kernels of corn and put them around the letters. That was supposed to help us learn them.

The rest of the time we would stitch with colored thread and draw on big sheets of paper with charcoal. Then at the end of the day the older children would take us home.

NEAR WAUKEGAN, ILLINOIS, 1910

We got all our schoolbooks free. But we had to buy a slate and a slate pencil to do our sums, and we needed a bottle of ink and a penholder and these steel pen points, and, of course, a copy book.

MARTHA'S VINEYARD, MASSACHUSETTS, 1895

There were places where you also had to buy your books, and that might come to five or six dollars a year, which was a sizeable sum in those days.

The first thing in the morning she would read to us. Usually it was a story or something like that. Then she would work with one grade at a time. She'd say, "Fourth grade, turn, rise, and pass." Then everybody in that grade—there might be four or five or just one—would go up to the recitation bench in front and sit there and recite their lesson. While they were reciting, you were supposed to be working on your lesson. But you'd also be kind of listening.

NEAR GREENE, IOWA, 1890

We'd have reading, writing, spelling, arithmetic, geography, and history. Each day toward the end we'd also have a spelling bee. Six or eight of us would stand up in front of the teacher's platform and she'd give us words to spell. Or we'd have a figure-down and we'd have problems to do in our heads. Of course, when you missed you had to drop out.

JACKSON COUNTY, MISSOURI, 1910

You'd finish the first reader, then go on to the second and the third and the fourth and so on. But you didn't get promoted automatically. It had nothing to do with your age. It depended on how far you got in your readers and your spellers and with your sums. You could stay in the fourth grade forever, and some did.

MOUNT CHASE, MAINE, 1900

In high school I had writing [penmanship] and literature all the way through. And I had history. And I had algebra, geometry, trigonometry, and physics. And I had Latin four years and Greek two and a half years. And I had art and choral music and everyday physical education.

For that I would get dressed up in this middy blouse and these very full dark blue bloomers and long black stockings and what we called "tennis shoes," little lightweight shoes with leather soles. Then we would do drills with Indian clubs and wands [long varnished sticks] and dumbbells.

DETROIT, 1905

SPEAKIN' PIECES

Every Friday afternoon we had speakin'. Everybody had some piece to recite, some famous poem or speech they had learned or just some funny stuff, whatever we wanted. This was to help us speak properly, not to be ashamed in front of the public.

FRANKLIN COUNTY, GEORGIA, 1895

63

*Many schools had such recitation periods. Children also recited
pieces on special occasions like the last day of school and the
Fourth of July, and at Christmas. There were thousands of these
pieces. Some came out of books. Others were just passed along.
Nobody knows who wrote them. But people remembered them.*

Ain't I glad I ain't a girl,
Hands to wash and hair to curl,
Skirts a-flappin' round my knees,
Ain't I glad that that ain't me.
Grandpa says it's just a chance
That I got to wearin' pants,
Says that when a kid is small,
They put dresses on 'em all.
They that kicks and makes a noise
Gets promoted into boys.
Them that sits and twists their curls,
They just leaves them, calls them "girls."

CHARLESTON, SOUTH CAROLINA, 1905

My little brother would get up at the front and he'd say,
"Lincoln was a great man, Washington was a great man, but
here, my friends, is a greater." Then he'd hold up a cheese
grater. His friends thought that was a riot.

INDIANAPOLIS, 1905

*Whooping cough then was a common disease among children. You
coughed rapidly, then ended up with a kind of whooping sound.
There was a very popular piece about it.*

Say, I've got the whooping cough—
Whoop! Whoop! Whoop!
Nearly shakes my poor head off—
Whoop! Whoop! Whoop!
Still it is a lot of fun

64

To see the other children run
Like I shot 'em with a gun
When they see me coming.
Whoop! Whoop! Whoop!

NEAR WAUKEGAN, ILLINOIS, 1910

Today most children are immunized against whooping cough, which is at least one reason why you don't hear this piece anymore.

Goliat vas a grate beeg fallow feefteen feet high. Day-veed vas a vary leetle fallow. He come up maybe yust to Goliat's knee. Goliat look at Dayveed an' he say, "Day-veed, I am goin' to keel you and eat you."

But Dayveed yust peek up fife stones. An' he put one of these een his sleeng an' he trow it at Goliat. An' vat do you tink happen? Dat stone heet Goliat in da stomick an' knock out all his brains.

SEATTLE, 1900

This is, of course, a version of the biblical story of David and Goliath. In his book Always the Young Strangers, *Carl Sandburg recalls an almost identical version he learned as a boy in Galesburg, Illinois. The dialect in this story makes fun of the way Swedish immigrants spoke. Such dialect stories were common at that time. Today they probably would be frowned upon.*

SPORTS

When I was in the eighth grade I was captain of the baseball team. That year we won the city championship. My dad helped to coach us. And we had a teacher name of Allie Blough, and she used to invite the team over to her house and give us fudge and hot chocolate. And the principal would give me advice on how to handle things, like if a player wanted to

65

chew tobacco, let him chew. When we won, the Chamber of Commerce had a luncheon to honor us, and they gave each of us a green and white sweater with the school's initial on it, "A" for Adams.

BALLARD, WASHINGTON, 1910

IF YOU DISOBEYED

If you acted up they'd stand you out on the floor. You'd have to stand there next to the teacher and look right at the class while she was teaching. One time a fella and I was lookin' at a picture of a camel, and he was tellin' me what fun it would be to get up on that hump and slide down into the hollow in its back. Well, that took us to laughin' and laughin', and we got stood out. We stood there for almost an hour. It was embarrassing.

PATTEN, MAINE, 1905

In parts of Virginia you were "stood up" instead of "stood out." That meant standing on one foot in a corner facing the wall.

If you talked in class and got caught, you'd get smacked with a ruler. The teacher'd come up to your seat and you'd hold out your hand, and she'd just let go as hard as she could.

SAN ANTONIO, TEXAS, 1905

I had this teacher at the Minor School named Miss Robble-bladt, and a boy had written a note about her and had passed it around the room. It said:

> "An eagle was flying south,
> With Miss Robblebladt in his mouth,
> When he found she was a fool,
> He dropped her at the Minor School."

Well, she saw it and got furious and finally discovered who did it and sent him to the principal. Then the principal sent him out to cut a switch and switched him with it. You could hear him howling all over the school.

SEATTLE, 1895

If you were switched in school that was considered part of your education. Usually your parents figured you deserved it, whether you did or not.

Our grammar school was very close to the Methodist Church, and in the top of that church there was a town clock. Well, in the winter at recess time we'd go out and throw snowballs at that clock. If you could get enough of 'em to stick, it would stop the hands. So this one day we were tryin' to do that, and the teacher saw us, and when we got back inside he got himself all worked up.

"You boys throwing snowballs at the Lord's building—dreadful, just dreadful!" he said.

Well, I hadn't done any more than the rest, but he kept lookin' at me. So I opened my big mouth and I said, "I wasn't throwin' 'em at the Lord's building. I was throwin' 'em at the town clock."

Boy, he took two strides down to where I was, and I went under the chair, and he grabbed for me and tore my shirt and hauled me out and let me have it.

I never forgave him for it. He had a nice grapevine, and one night I went up there with a gang of boys and we raided his old vine. And I vowed that when I grew up he was really goin' to hear something. But they moved away.

MARTHA'S VINEYARD, MASSACHUSETTS, 1895

I liked school until they got to whippin' me.
Why'd they whip you?
I'd wet my clothes. I was just six years old then, and I

67

couldn't help it. I had a note from the doctor to let me be excused, but the teacher wouldn't do it. Each time it happened he would switch me on my legs, and I would just cry and cry. My daddy said they weren't goin' to beat on me for somethin' I couldn't help. So he kept me home, and I never went again.

It was my sister who taught me. She'd say, "Come on, now. Let me learn ya somethin'." And she'd take up her book and sit me down, and we'd look at it, and she'd read it off to me. Then I had to read it back to her. She taught me to read a little and to write a little, and she taught me sums.

CARROLL COUNTY, GEORGIA, 1900

SOME OF US QUIT

I went until I was twelve years old. Then my folks wanted me to work. They needed the money. So I got a job in a drugstore. I made ten dollars a week, and I felt like a man.

NEWARK, NEW JERSEY, 1903

When I was sixteen I still had a way to go, but I wanted to quit and get a job. Well, we had a test one day, and I never wrote a word. The teacher asked me why, and I said, "I don't want to go to school anymore. I want to go to work."

About five o'clock that afternoon here was this teacher comin' over to my house. So I went down to the barn to get away. But she told my father what I had said, and when I got home he had a big talk with me.

He said, "You're wrong about school. You should keep goin'. Now when you go to bed tonight, you lay there and think about this, and you'll change your mind."

I said, "I want to work. I've got a job lined up."

He said, "I think you should stick to your schoolin'. Now in the morning I'm going to ask you your decision."

So when I got up he asked me, and I said, "I want to get

68

done." He said, "All right, if that's the way you feel, get done." So I went to work for a grocery.

MARTHA'S VINEYARD, MASSACHUSETTS, 1900

AUTOGRAPHS

When you were about to graduate it was the custom to buy an autograph album. Then your friends and relatives would write their good wishes in it, and whatever else occurred to them.

In your life may you find
Every cloud silver-lined.

BROOKLYN, NEW YORK, 1900

When Cupid sends his arrow home, I hope he Mrs. you.

HELENA, MONTANA, 1905

When you are sliding down the bannister of life, think of me as a splinter in your career.

ATLANTA, 1900

When you're old and think you're sweet,
Take off your shoes and smell your feet.

DETROIT, 1905

Love many, trust few,
Always paddle your own canoe.

NEAR STOCKTON, CALIFORNIA, 1900

GRADUATION

Our graduating class was the largest up to that time. There were thirty of us, and, of course, everybody was all dressed up. The boys had dark suits and ties, and the girls were all in white. I had this white organdy dress with a high collar and

69

long sleeves, and the skirt came down to my ankles, and it was all tucks and lace.

The Reverend Barr came out from Kansas City to conduct the religious service, and some of the students spoke, and the superintendent of schools gave the commencement address. Then they gave out the medals and the diplomas. At the end we gave our school call: "Independence High School! Rah! Rah! Rah!" Then it was over.

INDEPENDENCE, MISSOURI, 1909

After graduation we had a dance at the town hall. A boy took me and we had an orchestra from off the island. First we had a grand march all the way around the inside of the hall. After that we had waltzes and two-steps and quadrilles. Mostly we danced to popular songs, like "Shade of the Old Apple Tree." Remember that one? That was very popular.

DEER ISLE, MAINE, 1909

Did you learn much in school?
Yes, I think so. I learned the ABCs. I learned to read and write. I learned the multiplication table. And I learned poetry, quite a lot of poetry. One time I wrote on the blackboard:

"Look not mournfully into the past. It is gone.
Wisely improve the present. It is thine."

NEAR LATHROP, CALIFORNIA, 1900

Games We Played

The games in this chapter are just a few of the great many that children played around the turn of the century, but they are the ones the people I visited remember best. Mostly these are outdoor games. Kissing games are on pages 116–18. Children still play some of these games, but most seem to be things of the past.

We would break twigs off a tree, Y-shaped twigs, and these would be dolls. If the doll was going to be a white child, we would peel off the bark. If it was going to be black, we'd leave it on. Then we'd take a bit of cloth and make a tiny hole in it and push the cloth down to where the legs separated. That would be the skirt. Then we would take a smaller piece and make another hole and stick it on top for the hat. We'd take our dolls on Sunday school picnics in my brother's toy wagon. And we'd have tacky parties to see who could dress their doll the ugliest.

MARS HILL, NORTH CAROLINA, 1912

Some children had dolls their mothers cut from two pieces of cloth, then stitched together and stuffed with rags, sawdust, or Spanish moss. Some also had dolls with heads made of metal or bisque, which is a form of pottery. You could attach a homemade body to these, or you could buy a head with a body and a wardrobe and two or three wigs.

72

"COWBOYS AND INDIANS"

We played that quite a bit. We'd go to the picture shows and see the cowboys and Indians. Then we would come back and imitate them. But the Indians in those shows was too—you know, too brutal. So when we played, a lot of us wanted to be cowboys, but we had to divide up.

We'd give one side a head start and they'd hide, and the other side would try to capture 'em. And we'd run around the same as if we was on horses. But the cowboys would be shootin' with guns and the Indians would be using bows and arrows. Of course, if you caught a cowboy you'd scalp him. You'd make believe you would.

PENOBSCOT INDIAN VILLAGE, INDIAN ISLAND, MAINE, 1914

"WE WANT TO SEE MISS JONES"

One of the players is Miss Jones. Another is a lady who answers the door. Another is a ghost. The others are the chorus. They form a circle and the lady who answers the door stands in the center.

CHORUS: Knock, knock.

LADY: What do you want?

CHORUS: We want to see Miss Jones.

LADY: Today is Monday. Miss Jones is upstairs washing, washing, washing. You cannot see her today.

CHORUS: Knock, knock.

LADY: What do you want?

CHORUS: We want to see Miss Jones.

LADY: Today is Tuesday. Miss Jones is upstairs ironing, ironing, ironing. You cannot see her today.

On each of the following days there is a similar conversation. On Wednesday Miss Jones is mending. On Thursday she

73

is cleaning. On Friday she is shopping. On Saturday the children return once more.

CHORUS: Knock, knock.

LADY: What do you want?

CHORUS: We want to see Miss Jones.

LADY: Today is Saturday. Miss Jones has fallen down the cellar steps and she is hurt, hurt, hurt. You cannot see her today.

CHORUS: Knock, knock.

LADY: What do you want?

CHORUS: We want to see Miss Jones.

LADY: Today is Sunday. Miss Jones is dead, dead, dead. You cannot see her today.

With this news, the children and the lady cry, and the children leave.

In the next scene Miss Jones is lying on the ground. She is in her grave, and the lady and the children march around the grave crying, "Poor Miss Jones! She is dead, dead, dead!"

Then all at once the ghost comes running out. He has come to pick Miss Jones' bones. But actually he tickles her until she manages to escape. Then he chases the children. The first one he catches is the next to play Miss Jones.

MARS HILL, NORTH CAROLINA, 1912

This game has many versions and many names. It also is called "Miss Jennia Jones," "Jenny Jones," and "Jenny Ann Jones." In Scotland, it is called "Janet Jo." In some versions, such as the one above, the words are spoken. In others they are sung.

"HOT HANDKERCHIEF"

A circle of players would sit on the ground, and one person sat in the center, and he had a handkerchief. And he would throw that handkerchief to one of the other players. Then that player would throw it to somebody else and so on. Meanwhile the one in the center would try to intercept it. If he did, the one who had just thrown it would take his place.

CHICO, CALIFORNIA, 1905

RHYMES FOR JUMP ROPE

The spring of every year there was jump rope.
Do you remember the rhymes?
Can't now. They just won't come. I reckon if I started jumpin' like an old fool they might.

LEXINGTON, VIRGINIA

> "Solomon Grundy,
> Born on Monday,
> Married on Tuesday,
> Took sick on Wednesday,
> Got worse on Thursday,
> Died on Friday,
> Buried on Saturday,
> Then came Sunday—
> And the end of Solomon Grundy."

For each day we'd raise the rope higher. Then at the end, after he died, we would turn it faster and faster.

NEW ORLEANS, 1910

> "Lady, lady, turn around,
> Lady, lady, touch the ground,

75

Lady, lady, touch your shoe,
Lady, lady, twenty-three skiddoo."

As you jumped you followed the directions. Then with "twenty-three skiddoo," you jumped out, and another girl jumped in.

NEAR STOCKTON, CALIFORNIA, 1910

"I had a letter from Nellie,
And what do you think it said?
Nellie had a baby, and its hair was red.
Now, how many hairs were in that head?"

You jumped until you missed, and the number of jumps was the number of hairs, and the one with the most hairs was the winner.

SEATTLE, 1905

They'd put the rope higher and higher and higher, and you had to jump over it. Then if you could, they'd do "SALT! PEPPER! MUSTARD! VINEGAR!—HOT!" First they'd turn it very slowly. Then at "HOT!" they'd take off, turn it as fast as they could.

ATLANTA, 1900

A RHYME FOR COUNTING OUT

Everybody would stand in a circle except for one, and he stood in the center and recited this rhyme:

"William, William Trembletoe,
Catches hens,
Puts them in pens,
Wire, briar, limberlock,

76

Twelve geese in a flock,
Some flew east, some flew west,
Some flew over the old crow's nest."

With each word he pointed to one person and moved around and around the circle until the rhyme was done. The last one he pointed to was It.

AUGUSTA, GEORGIA, 1895

Another version ends with "Some flew over the cuckoo's nest."

"BLACK MAN"

We would choose one player to be the black man. He would stand out there in the middle of a field, and the rest of us would line up at one end. Then he'd call out, "What are you doing in my field?"

We'd say, "Stealing grapes."

He'd ask, "What will you do when the black man comes?"

We'd say, "Rush right through like we always do."

Then we'd rush across the field toward the other side. As we came by, he tried to tag as many as he could. And the ones he tagged also became black men and stayed out there with him. We would try to get by them again and again until all of us had been caught and all of us were black men. The last one to be caught was the first black man in the next game.

HELENA, MONTANA

JACKSON COUNTY, MISSOURI

SHANNON CITY, IOWA

1900–1910

In some places this game was called "Pom Pom Pullaway." The player who was It would call, "Pom pom pullaway. If you don't come, I'll pull you away." Then the players would rush across the field. In the winter this game was also played on ice skates.

"LEMONADE"

There would be two teams, and they would be twenty, twenty-five feet apart. The other team would ask us, "Where you from?"

We'd say, "New York."

Then they'd ask, "What's your trade?"

We'd say, "Lemonade."

And they'd say, "Give us some."

And we'd say, "If you can run."

Then they'd say, "Go to work!"

So both teams would stand out in the middle, and our team would make believe we were shoveling dirt or driving a buggy or whatever. And they'd try to guess what we were doing. To make it easier, we'd give them the first letters of each word, like "S.D." for shoveling dirt.

If they guessed wrong we'd chase 'em back to their base and catch as many as we could, then have another turn. If they guessed right, they'd chase us. Then it was their turn. We played until everybody on one side was captured.

NEAR STOCKTON, CALIFORNIA, 1910

This game had many names. Along with "Lemonade," it was called "New York," "Philadelphia," "New Orleans," "Trades," "Dumb Trades," and "Pretty Girls' Station."

"PRISONERS' BASE"

There would be two teams facing each other across a street, and the street itself was No-Man's-Land. The idea was to go out there and capture as many members of the other team as you could. You did that by tagging them. But you could only tag somebody who was out there before you were.

To start, one team would send out a player to taunt the other team, to get them a little riled up. He'd just stand out there and insult them. Well, soon they'd send somebody out to capture him, and he'd try to get back to his base. Meanwhile, somebody else from his team would come out and try to tag the fella who was chasing him. Then somebody from the *other* team would come out, and so on.

If you got captured they'd put you in a prison they had marked out behind their line. But if one of your men slipped through, he could free you. If there were a lot of prisoners, you'd all hold hands to form a chain that reached out into No-Man's-Land. Then if the player at the end of the line was freed, you'd all be free. When everybody on one team was captured, that was the game.

SAN FRANCISCO, 1910

As that chain of prisoners reached farther into the street, the game became dangerous, for the chain blocked the path of delivery wagons and ice wagons pulled by fast-moving horses.

"DUCK ON A ROCK"

We'd find a boulder or a post or something that stood up about three feet off the ground, and we'd put a fair-sized rock on it. We called that rock a "duck." Then we'd each find another rock and take turns throwing our rocks at the duck, trying to knock it off its perch. The first one to do so was the winner.

BANGOR, MAINE, 1910

"SHINNY"

This was like hockey, except that we played in the street and we used a beat-up tin can for a puck and everybody had a branch or a stick to hit it with. The idea was to hit the can across the other team's goal line. Every time we scored we yelled, "Shin-neeeee!"

DETROIT, 1905

Sometimes players would use a block of wood or a rubber ball instead of a can, and instead of sticks they'd use their feet. North American Indians also played a version of this game.

"MUMBLY-PEG"

You needed a flat piece of ground and a pocket knife with two blades. You'd have the big blade straight out and the small blade turned at a right angle. Then you'd hold the knife between your thumb and your first finger and gently flip it up into the air away from you. If the big blade stuck straight in the ground, you'd get five points. If the little blade went straight in and the handle stood straight out, you'd get ten points. If both blades went in, you got fifteen. The first one to get a hundred points was the winner.

WOODWARD COUNTY, OKLAHOMA, 1910

There was another version of this game that was far more complicated. It involved performing at least twenty tricks with your knife. Some of the people I visited recalled sliding a knife off the palm of a hand so it would stick in the ground, or flipping it from a shoulder or wrist. But nobody remembered the whole game. The best description I have seen of it takes twenty-one pages. It is in a book by Robert Paul Smith called How to Do Nothing with Nobody All Alone by Yourself *(W. W. Norton & Company, 1958).*

"TIP CAT"

There'd be a pitcher, a batter, a cat, and a bat. The cat was a piece of wood four or five inches long. Often it was cut from a broomstick. You'd whittle each end to a point so it looked something like this:

The players would draw a circle on the ground a foot or two across. The batter would stand next to the circle, and the pitcher would stand about fifteen or twenty feet away. Then the pitcher would try to throw the cat into the circle, but the batter would try to keep it out by blocking it with his bat.

If the cat landed inside, the batter lost his turn and changed places with the pitcher. If it landed outside, he would hit it on one of the ends with his bat, which would make it fly high into the air. Then before it reached the ground, he would hit it again as hard as he could.

If the pitcher caught it, the batter was out. But if he got it by the pitcher, the batter had to guess how many feet it had traveled, for each foot added one point to his score. After he guessed, the pitcher measured the actual distance with the length of his foot. If the batter's guess was too high, he didn't get any points. If he was too low, he got the number he guessed.

Then they changed places. Usually they played seven innings, or until one of them had a certain number of points.

DETROIT

AUGUSTA, GEORGIA

CAMBRIDGE, MASSACHUSETTS

1895–1910

81

GAMES WITH A BALL

In some places you could buy a ball. But it wasn't always easy to get one, and often they cost more than you could afford. So many children made their own, or one of their parents or a teacher helped them make one.

To make a ball we'd get an old sock beyond patching and unravel it and wind the yarn tightly around a walnut or a stone. Then your mother'd take a big needle and a lot of thread, and stitch around and through and around and through until it held. Of course, if you gave it a few hard licks you'd have to do some repair work.

ALBANY, GEORGIA, 1900

Instead of yarn, some children used string and wrapped their ball in tape. Or they used rag balls. They'd take an old stocking and stuff part of it with rags until it was hard. Then they'd cut off the rest and sew up the opening. Some even used hog bladders. The biggest, strongest ones came from the oldest hogs. If you could get one, you'd blow it up and tie it off with a string, and you'd have a really good ball.

"ANTNEY OVER"

There'd be a bunch of us in front of the house and a bunch of us in back of the house, and we'd throw the ball back and forth over the roof. Each time somebody threw it, he'd call, "Antney over!" to let them know it was coming. If somebody caught it on the fly, he'd slip around to the other side and try to hit one of their players with the ball. If he did, he'd bring him back. The side that ended up with all the players was, of course, the winner.

FINCASTLE, VIRGINIA, 1905

To play this game, you needed a small building with a lot of space around it—a small barn, shed, school, or house. So it was a game most often played in the country or in a small town. It had many other names: "Over the Barn," "House Over," "Hailey Over" (which may come from "Hail ye! over!") and "Anthony Over" —and from this "Antney Over."

"ONE OLD CAT"

There would be a pitcher and a batter. The pitcher would keep pitching the ball until the batter hit it. When he did, the batter would run from home plate to the pitcher's base and back again. If he made it all the way, it counted as a run, and he batted again. But if the pitcher caught the ball on the fly, or if he picked it up and hit the batter with it, or tagged him, the batter was out. Then they changed places. Games would last for nine innings or seven innings, or until somebody had to go home.

DETROIT, 1910

When each side had two players, the game was called "Two Old Cat." Usually there would be a pitcher and a fielder on one side, and a batter and a catcher on the other side.

"ROLY POLY"

Three or four of us would play. We each would dig a small hole in the ground, and these holes would be in a line about three feet apart. Then we would take turns rolling a ball down the line of holes. If the ball dropped into one of the holes, the player whose hole it was grabbed the ball and threw it at another player. If he hit him, he'd drop a stone in that player's hole. If he missed, he'd put one in his own hole.

The first player to get three stones stood facing a tree or a wall and heaved the ball backward over his shoulder. Then the rest of us lined up where the ball landed, and he bent over, and we each fired the ball at his bottom three times. If anybody missed, even once, they changed places with him, and he took three shots at them.

BOSTON, 1905

GAMES WITH MARBLES

A player might have three or four kinds of marbles. There were "aggies," which were made from the mineral agate and were the most beautiful and the most expensive. There were "steelies," which were small ball bearings. There were "realies" or "glassies," made from glass, and "Chinees," small white marbles made from a kind of porcelain, and "jugs," made from chalk or clay. And there were others. Each kind had many names.

Often an agate or a steelie was used as a shooter or a "taw." To decide who would go first in a game and the order in which others would follow, the players usually marked a "taw line" in the dirt or on the sidewalk. Then they shot or tossed a marble toward this line. The one whose marble came closest was the first to shoot, the one who was next would be second, and so on.

Most children played marbles for keeps. But some could not do that because their families disapproved of gambling. If they wanted to play, they had to find players who would give them back their marbles when the game was over.

"RING TAW"

We'd draw a big circle in the dirt, probably six feet across, and each of us would put in four, five marbles. The idea was to knock out as many marbles as you could, since you kept

84

everything you knocked out. The only marble you couldn't shoot at was some other player's taw.

The first time you shot was from the taw line. Then you shot from wherever you were. You kept shooting until you missed, and you kept playing until all the marbles had been knocked out. Sometimes a crowd of kids would be watching, and one of them would holler, *"¡La bola!"*—that means "riot"—and they'd all dive in and grab your marbles and disappear. That also would end the game.

TUCSON, ARIZONA, 1900

"RING HOLE"

We'd dig this hole about the size of a dinner plate, and everybody would put two, three marbles around the edge. Then each of us would shoot from the taw line and whatever we knocked in was ours.

NEW YORK, UPPER EAST SIDE DISTRICT, 1895

A MARBLE BOARD

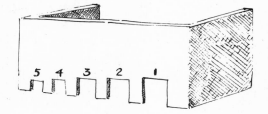

Almost everybody had a marble board. You could win a lot of marbles with one of those. You'd cut it out of the side of an apple box or somethin' like that. Then you'd make little notches at the bottom and put a number over each one. That would be the number of marbles somebody won if he could

85

get his marble through the hole. Then you might put sides on your board and hinges, so that it would stand up and later you could fold it.

If a kid wanted to play, I'd set my marble board on the ground, and he'd back off four or five feet and try to shoot a marble through one of the holes. If he won, he got my marbles. If he missed, I got his. Then I'd stick my board under my arm and go find somebody else to play.

CAMBRIDGE, MASSACHUSETTS, 1905

Other Things We Did

SWIMMING

Where the creek emptied into the river there was a great hole in the riverbed. And in the summer the water in that hole would be really warm. Up above the hole there was this ledge of rocks. I'd take my clothes off and dive from there.

CASCADE COUNTY, MONTANA, 1914

This hotel was right down near the water, and they had an orchestra that played out of doors. We would go down there on the streetcar and sit on the beach and sometimes go paddling. We'd take off our shoes and socks and turn up our skirts and tie them tight around to keep our petticoats from getting wet. Then we'd let the waves wash over our feet and we'd listen to the music.

BROOKLYN, NEW YORK, 1900

FISHING

We never had very much of a fishing outfit—just a willow branch for a pole, and ordinary wrapping twine for line, and some old hooks. For bait we'd find some grasshoppers. Then we'd go down to this creek and fish. What we couldn't catch with a hook, we'd chase between the rocks and grab with our hands.

CASCADE COUNTY, MONTANA, 1914

A number of people said that a good straight sapling—an ash, an alder, a birch, a willow—also made a good "wood stick pole." They would find one about eight or nine feet long and cut off all the branches. Then they would cut a line as long as the pole and tie it to the fishing end. If they ever needed to shorten the line, they'd just wrap more of it around the end and secure it with a half hitch.

BIKING

Nobody I talked to had a bicycle with a coaster brake or a set of hand brakes. The latest advance was the chain drive. If you had one, you could stop by pedaling backwards. Otherwise, you stopped by putting your feet down and dragging them on the ground. If you wanted somebody to get out of the way, you blew a whistle you wore around your neck, or you sounded a bell on your handlebar. This was a bell you wound up like a watch, and it rang until it

88

*ran down. In those days a bicycle usually wasn't called a "bike."
It was called a "wheel."*

READING

My father used to read to us from *The Youth's Companion*.
Sometimes it was a continued story, and we could hardly
wait for the mail to bring the next issue so we could go on
with it.

BUCKLEY, ILLINOIS, 1905

Every week I'd buy the *Tip Top Weekly* at the drugstore in
town. It was about these Tip Tops, Frank and Dick Merriwell,
these college guys who were real good athletes and real hon-
orable fellows, and the adventures they were always having.
At night my sister would read the stories aloud, and the whole
family would listen.

NEAR GREENE, IOWA, 1905

The Youth's Companion for All the Family *probably was
the most popular children's magazine in the country. It appeared
every week from 1827 to 1929. Frank and Dick Merriwell were
students at Yale University, where they were expert athletes and
brilliant scholars. They also were rich, charming, and popular.
But they had enemies, too, and each week they outwitted at least
a few. Their adventures appeared in* Tip Top Weekly *for
seventeen years starting in 1896.*

In the backyard there was a small elm tree, and I would
climb up into that tree and sit there and read by the hour. I
read *Little Women* there and the "Little Colonel" books and
the "Elsie Dinsmore" books. I liked to read about girls who
had everything, and in books most of them did. But we didn't.
There was a girl in town I always thought of as the Little

89

Colonel. She was that beautiful and that good and that rich and that everything.

The "Little Colonel" books were about a girl named Lloyd and her experiences growing up in a mansion in Kentucky. Lloyd was that beautiful, that good, that rich, that everything.

Elsie Dinsmore, on the other hand, might be regarded today as a pain in the neck. Her great interest was in getting people to behave properly, particularly adults. But the books about her were very popular. In all, twenty-six were published.

These books were, of course, intended for girls. Many boys in that period were reading the historical adventure stories George A. Henty was writing. They also were reading Ragged Dick *and other novels by Horatio Alger in which young men overcame great handicaps to win wealth and honor.*

Father had a big library with all sorts of books, and I read almost everything he had. And there was a book called *Sappho*, I think it was, by a French author, and I got very interested in this *Sappho* business. But Father thought it was a little off color, and he said I had no business reading such books. And I said I thought I could read anything he could read. If it was all right for him to read, why wasn't it all right for me? And he said, "Because I say so."

Sappho was one of the great poets of ancient Greece. She lived on the island of Lesbos with a group of young women. The term "lesbian" derives from the name of the island.

At least once a week I would ride the streetcar five miles into the city, and I would spend the whole time at the library reading. It was one of the nicest places I knew. There were two large rooms. One was for magazines and the other was for books. They had every magazine I had ever heard of, and every book. Coming in from that small town out there, it was really something.

LINCOLN, NEBRASKA, 1905

RIDDLING

We used to bone up on them, call them out to one another as a challenge. . . .

LEXINGTON, VIRGINIA

The answers to these riddles are on page 102.

1.   A riddle, a riddle, as I suppose
   A thousand eyes and never a nose.

TUCSON, ARIZONA, 1900

2. What goes up a chimney down, but won't go up a chimney up? And what comes down a chimney down, but won't go down the chimney up?

NEW YORK, UPPER EAST SIDE DISTRICT, 1900

3. On a hill there is a mill, and around this mill there is a walk, and on this walk there is a key. What place is this?

SAN FRANCISCO, 1895

4. What is more wonderful than a dog that can count?

DETROIT, 1905

5. What three words did Adam use when he introduced himself to Eve? They read the same backward and forward.

AUGUSTA, GEORGIA, 1895

91

6. What is the difference between a schoolboy and a post-age stamp?

7. What is the difference between a watchmaker and a jailer?

SAN ANTONIO, TEXAS, 1905

8. When is a door not a door?

9. Why is a lady like a hinge?

STOCKTON, CALIFORNIA, 1900

10. Why is a young dog who is slow on his feet like a sheet of writing paper?

BOULDER, COLORADO, 1910

11.   Little Nanny Etticoat
    With a white petticoat
    And a red nose,
    The longer she stands,
    The shorter she grows.
    What is she?

12.   As I was passing London Hall,
    I heard a fellow so loudly call,
    His lips were bone, his toes were horn,
    And this fellow was never born.
    Who or what is he?

BUNKERVILLE, NEVADA, 1910

13.   Twelve pears were hanging high,
    Twelve men were riding by,
    Each took a pear
    And left eleven hanging there.
    Who took the pear?

STONINGTON, MAINE, 1895

14. On this hill there was a green house. And inside the green house there was a white house. And inside the

white house there was a red house. And inside the red house there were a lot of little blacks and whites sittin' there. What place is this?

BEDFORD COUNTY, TENNESSEE, 1895

15. This hobo sat on top of a moving freight train, but his feet dragged on the ground. Who was he?

OAK CREEK, ARIZONA, 1910

RHYMES AND OTHER FOOLISHNESS

Whisperin' is lying, lying is a sin,
When you go to Heaven they won't let you in.

WEIMAR, TEXAS, 1895

It is a sin to steal a pin,
It is a greater to steal a potater.

ATLANTA, 1895

Roses are red, cabbage is green,
You have a head like a lima bean.

CAMBRIDGE, MASSACHUSETTS, 1900

If I was as ugly as you, I'd sue my mother and father.

SEATTLE, 1910

Do you carrot all for me?
My heart beets for you,
With your turnip nose,
And your radish lips, you are a peach.
If we cantaloupe, lettuce marry.
We'd make a swell pear.

DETROIT, 1905

There's nobody home but the sofa, and that's just lounging around.

There's nobody home but the stove, and that's just gone out.

BROOKLYN, NEW YORK, 1900

TAKING LESSONS

A lady came out every week from Marble Rock to give me lessons on this old pedal organ we had. She had pupils all over the countryside and drove a horse and buggy from one farm to another. She would come once a week for an hour. Mostly it was scales we did, but to keep my interest up sometimes she'd give me hymns to play.

NEAR GREENE, IOWA, 1900

On Saturday mornings we would go into town for our elocution lessons. There were about ten of us whose mothers were interested in that sort of thing, and this lady would come over from San Francisco to teach us. Every week she would give us something to memorize. Usually it was a poem of olden times long ago by Longfellow or Whittier or one of those. Then the next week we would get up on the stage, and she would tell us how to walk, how to stand, how to conduct ourselves, and how to say that poem, the kind of expression to use and so forth. This was supposed to give us social poise and confidence.

STOCKTON, CALIFORNIA, 1905

This very old lady, Miss Bell, taught us to dance. Every week we'd meet at somebody else's house where they had a big room and a piano. There'd be almost twenty of us, mostly ten, eleven years old. The girls would have on these stiff white dresses and big pink sashes, and the boys would be wearing sailor suits. Miss Bell would teach us round dances and the waltz and the two-step. Then she showed us how to ask a girl to dance, and how to hold her so you wouldn't wrinkle her dress, and what to do when the dance was over. It was heels together, hands folded in front, and bow from the waist.

AUGUSTA, GEORGIA, 1895

MAKING ALDER WHISTLES

Up back of the school there were a lot of alders, and in the spring of the year I'd go up there with a jackknife and make alder whistles. Of course, you also could use willow wood, if you had any, or poplar or cedar, or anything soft. But you had to do it when the sap was rising and the bark was loose.

First, you'd cut off a piece of wood about an inch thick and a little longer than your finger. Then you'd try to get the bark off in one piece. You'd make a cut two-thirds of the way back and all the way around. Then to loosen the bark you'd tap it gently here and there with your knife, and by 'n' by you'd be able to ease it off.

SLIDE OFF GENTLY

CUT IN BARK ALL THE WAY AROUND

Once you got the bark off, you'd cut these two notches up front where the whistle was going to be.

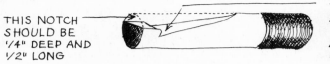

THIS NOTCH SHOULD BE 1/4" DEEP AND 1/2" LONG

THIS NOTCH SHOULD BE 1/2" DEEP HERE AND 1" TO 1 1/2" LONG

Then you'd slip the bark back on and cut a little hole in it over the deepest notch for the sound to get out.

95

BLOW THROUGH → HERE

CUT NOTCH IN BARK

Then you'd have a whistle.

STONINGTON, MAINE, 1895

To make a twig doll, see page 72; a yarn ball, page 82; a marble board, page 85; a fishing pole, page 88; a Hallowe'en tick tack, page 128.

RAISING A PIG

My father had this little pig, and I asked him if I could have it for my own. He said, "If you feed him." Well, I did. And every week I cleaned his pen, and every week I washed him in buttermilk, and he was just as white and handsome. And, you know, he got to be quite a big pig. Then all at once it was slaughtering time and Father killed him. What did I do? I went up to my room and hid my head in the feather bed. I shed tears over that. After that I didn't want any more little pigs.

PATTEN, MAINE, 1900

SMOKING

The sailing vessel referred to below carried cargo up and down the Atlantic coast. Since the captain of this vessel was away much of the time, each summer when school was out his wife and young son left their home in Deer Isle, Maine, and traveled with him.

96

I was about ten that year, and we were comin' up from Georgia with a load of lumber. On the forward hatch we had this lifeboat, and there was room enough so you could crawl up in the bow of her, and nobody'd see ya. So one day they missed me. They looked all over the vessel, and they hollered and hollered, and I didn't answer. So Mother fainted away. And Father went and grabbed some water out of a bilge pump and throwed it on her and brought her to. Then one of the sailors happened to look in that lifeboat, and he says, "Here he is under here, smoking a cigarette." But it was just a piece of paper I was trying out.

OFF THE ATLANTIC COAST, 1905

A great many boys were interested in smoking, but most couldn't get tobacco. So they tried coffee grounds, dried sunflower seeds, corn silk, cornmeal, corn husks, fern husks, alfalfa, string, or other things. They'd wrap it in paper, then hide somewhere and try to smoke it. By the time they were twelve or thirteen, some were taking their father's Bull Durham or Duke's Mixture tobacco and sneaking off and rolling real cigarettes.

Few girls, if any, tried smoking, but there were some who dipped snuff. Snuff is a powdered tobacco that comes in different flavors. In those days people dipped it from a snuff can with a brush or a stick. Then they put it between their gum and their cheek, or they rubbed it on their teeth. They said using it helped them relax.

One woman I visited in Georgia started dipping snuff when she was a young child. Her mother introduced her to it. "I carried a box of it wherever I went," she said. "When I went to work in the fields, I'd take it along. It kept me from gettin' hungry, and it made me feel easier."

FIGHTING

These immigrant boys would come over from this other neighborhood and push us around and take our things. So I called the fellows together and we had a little meeting, about ten or twelve of us, and we organized a gang to protect ourselves. The Seventh Avenue Gang we called it. We all got whistles, and if anybody started to molest you, you blew your whistle. Then all the fellows who were around would come rushing out and knock the spots out of them.

BROOKLYN, NEW YORK, 1895

USING DIRTY WORDS

We'd say anything. All the bodily functions—piss, shit, all that was everyday conversation. Except when girls were around. We all were very careful not to use dirty words in front of girls.

NEAR SEBASTOPOL, CALIFORNIA, 1905

GOING TO A SHOW

When a medicine wagon came to town, that night they'd give a free show right on the street. They'd set out [gasoline] flares so we could see. Then they'd get up on the back of their wagon and play on a mandolin and sing and joke around and do stunts like stand on their heads. After that they'd try to sell some medicine that cured whatever ailed you—nerve pills, worm cakes, liquor cure, all sorts of stuff.

FORT SMITH, ARKANSAS, 1910

Two, three times a year a minstrel show would come through, and we'd always go. There'd be a row of white men up on the stage made up to look like black men. They'd tell jokes and do different acts and play the banjo and dance and sing. They'd sing "Under the Bamboo Tree," and sometimes they'd sing this:

"Oh, money is the milk in the coconut,
Oh, money is the milk in the jug,
When you got lots of money,
You feel very funny,
And as snug as a bug in a rug."

I liked that.

SHANNON CITY, IOWA, 1900

That song was called "Money." The other song, "Under the Bamboo Tree," tells of a love affair in an African jungle. The chorus goes: "If you lak-a-me lak I lak-a-you and we lak-a-both the same, / I lak-a-say, this very day, I lak-a-change your name, / 'Cause I love-a-you and love-a-you true. . . ."

The first minstrel men actually were black slaves who performed on plantations where they worked. Then white entertainers picked up their routines and began performing them in public. The whites dressed in gaudy costumes and wore blackface—black makeup with white rings around the eyes and mouth. They portrayed blacks as lazy, ignorant fools.

After the slaves were freed, those who wanted to be entertainers found that the only jobs for them were in minstrel shows. But in these shows they had to wear the same makeup whites wore, and they had to behave like the fools whites made them out to be.

Saturday afternoons they'd have these melodramas downtown. In every one there would be a hero who was practically perfect, and he would have a girl friend who also was. And there would be a villain who was interested in her, but she wouldn't be interested in him. So the hero would try to pro-

99

tect her from the villain, and they would have all these fistfights and duels. Then the villain would decide to kill her. But in the end she would be rescued.

There was this one play in which the villain took her to a sawmill and strapped her to this long board, and the board started moving toward this great round saw. And she got closer and closer, but he just stood there smiling in this evil way, and all of us were hissing and screaming at him. Then the hero rode right onto the stage on this horse—and we were all hollering and cheering—and he shot the villain dead and rescued her just in time.

CHICO, CALIFORNIA, 1900

Melodramas were very popular at that time. They were performed by traveling companies almost everywhere.

For a nickel we would go to the Happy Hour on Sunday afternoons. That was the movie theater in our neighborhood. Whole gangs of us would go and sit on benches and watch the silent movies. Mostly these were comedies we saw.

There was one in which this man stopped in a grocery store and bought a piece of cake to eat. And there was a man next to him washing the window with a sponge. Well, instead of picking up his cake, he picked up the sponge by mistake and ate it, and he didn't know the difference.

Then to wash it down he drank two or three bottles of pop, and because of the sponge in his stomach he began to swell up like he was pregnant. So they put sacks of flour on top of him to make his stomach go down, and the pop started squirtin' out of his ears. . . .

NEW ORLEANS, 1914

Silent movies were introduced in about 1900. Printed titles were flashed on the screen to explain what was going on, and during the movie usually somebody played a piano or an organ to help set the mood. "Talkies" arrived in 1927.

TAKING A TRIP

I think Aunt Al was the one who started talking about going to Yosemite Park. "It would be nice to go to Yosemite," she said. Now that was a long trip. It was a hundred and twenty-five miles by the Big Oak Flat Road. But we went anyway. We took this little camp wagon that had a canvas top on it, and we had two horses pulling. There was my sister Alicia, my sister Theodosia, my Aunt Al, Mother, and me. It took us seven days.

I drove and Mother sat next to me. Everybody else sat in the back on this big bale of hay we'd brought along for the horses. But when we started uphill into the mountains there was too much weight for them. So everybody got out and walked but me. That was one thing that slowed us down.

Another thing was that Mother was being so careful with the horses. When we started getting up into the mountains, the water in the streams was cold and she wouldn't let them drink it. She said they were valley horses and it would make 'em sick. So whenever they needed a drink we'd stop and she'd build a fire and warm the water up.

That was the first year they allowed cars in Yosemite. If you brought a car in, you had to stop at the ranger station and pick up a ranger and drive to your camp. Then he'd put your car in a garage, and it stayed there until you were ready to leave. But we took our wagon right in, rode the horses all over the place.

EAST OF STOCKTON, CALIFORNIA, 1914

1. A kitchen sieve.
2. An umbrella.
3. Milwaukee.
4. A spelling bee.
5. "Madam, I'm Adam."
6. One you lick with a stick. The other you stick with a lick.
7. One sells watches. The other watches cells.
8. When it's ajar (a jar).
9. She is something to adore (a door).
10. A young dog who is slow on his feet is a slow pup. A slow pup is a slope up. A slope up is an inclined plane. An inclined plane is an ink-lined plane. An ink-lined plane is a sheet of writing paper.
11. A candle.
12. A rooster. He was hatched, not born.
13. A man named Each.
14. A watermelon.
15. Longfellow.

If I Did Something Wrong

We had been throwing rocks at the streetlights and knocking them out. But somebody saw us and told my father about it. When I got home he said, "What in the world were you doin' that for? Don't you have any sense at all? Get out to the woodshed!" So I went out there with him, and he took me by the scruff of the neck and took up a stick and just walloped away, laid on twenty, thirty licks as hard as he could. I cried like the devil. When he finished, he looked at me and said, "If you ever do anything like that again, I'll whip you within an inch of your life. I mean it." I was black and blue for a week.

LYNCHBURG, VIRGINIA, 1912

My parents used to jaw me if I did something wrong, but I never got a lickin'. Oh, if I was gettin' kind of hateful and Mother had a thimble on her finger, she'd crack me on top of the head with it. But that was all.

MOUNT CHASE, MAINE, 1900

There was a hill of clay right next to town, and out of this clay we made what we called "mud daubs." You'd roll the clay up into a little ball, and wet it, and stick it on the end of a willow branch. Then you'd swing that branch back and whip it forward and that clay would go quite a distance.

Well, the miller wasn't too popular with us boys, and sometimes we would mud daub his flour mill, and now and then we'd break a window. If I was involved, he'd go to my father and tell him. So then my father would say to me, "Now listen, you will have to repay him for his window, but you also will have to ask him for his forgiveness."

That wasn't easy, you know, to go to a person like that and tell him you are sorry for what you have done and ask him to forgive you. It wasn't easy at all.

ORDERVILLE, UTAH, 1900

Strangers

The first time I saw Indians they were coming up the river near our house in a big canoe. I had read in stories how they would kill you and scalp you. So I ran and hid.

NEAR FLORENCE, WASHINGTON, 1910

The first time I saw a white person I was about five years old. My uncle went into town for provisions and I went along. I rode behind him on his horse, but when we got there I began to cry. He told me, "Stop crying! People are looking at us." I said, "I can't help it. I want to go home." It was very strange to see these people with white faces, to see how they dressed and how they were doing things.

PAPAGO INDIAN VILLAGE NEAR TUCSON, ARIZONA, 1905

Once or twice every summer Gypsies would drive down the road that went past our farm. They'd have maybe ten, twelve wagons all painted up in gay colors, and often they would have a bear tied to the end. They'd come along real slow and when they got to our house they'd leave their wagons and come to visit. They always wanted to tell our fortunes. Then, if they had a bear, they'd bring him along, and they'd play on a fiddle and he'd dance with one of them. When they left, Mother would give them a couple of pies or a chicken. If we weren't nice to them, she was afraid they'd steal somethin' or burn the barn down.

NEAR DETROIT, 1900

It was in that period that Gypsies began arriving from Europe. A thousand years before they had migrated from India to Persia, and then they spread in many directions. They traveled in small groups, moving from place to place, working as fortune-tellers, musicians, horse traders, and peddlers.

A lot of tramps were coming through, stealin' rides on the freight trains or just walkin'. Some were regular bums. Others were young people out to see the country. Often they'd come around back and knock on the door and ask for food. They would say, "Is there a little work I can do for somethin' to eat?" and my mother would give them a sandwich, and they'd stand out there and eat it. Then maybe she'd have them sweep off the porch or something. Everybody said that if you gave them anything they'd put a mark on your house. Then the other tramps would know where to try. But I never could find one.

TUCSON, ARIZONA, 1910

On Sundays the Poles who worked in the factories would come out into the country for a picnic with their families. Sometimes they would come into our cow lot on the river and have a real lively time, which we never had, not like that. Then a few came out and bought this farm two down from ours. And they sent their children to our one-room school, and there were problems about that. And they built themselves a small church, and there was grumbling about that. Then on Sundays they would have their friends out from the city and have big picnics over there. The farmer next to them didn't like that at all, and he would patrol his property line with a shotgun. Somehow we picked up the idea that city people and ethnic people were dangerous and bad.

NEAR WAUKEGAN, ILLINOIS, 1910

We went to the Catholic school in town, so each morning we had to walk by the public school. The kids there would yell, "Cat licker! Pot licker! Cat licker! Pot licker!" I wanted to say, "Why are you doing that?" but I was afraid to.

KALAMAZOO, MICHIGAN, 1910

There was this one colored boy who was our age. His mother was somebody's cook. He was a good athlete and we liked him, and we played football with him quite a lot. But it wasn't the usual thing to mix that way. It really wasn't a common thing. So if we were going to somebody's house to play, we would never invite him. Of course, it never occurred to him that we would. He would just go on his way.

LEXINGTON, VIRGINIA, 1914

Our Social Life

VISITING

If people wanted to visit in those days, they didn't have to be invited. They'd just come by.

The women in town came to call in the afternoon. Usually it was after two o'clock. So if Mother was going to be home, she always had to be prepared. If somebody did come by, they'd have tea and sit and talk for an hour or so. If the conversation wasn't too private, sometimes they'd invite me to join them.

When she left, she'd leave a calling card with her name on it. That was to remind us that now it was our turn to visit her. All the women in town had these cards. If they came to call and we weren't home, they'd just leave their cards under the door.

INDEPENDENCE, MISSOURI, 1910

In the evening the boys we knew came to call. They'd just drive into the yard and unhitch their horses, and we'd invite them in. Then we'd sit around and gab, or we'd play cards. Or one of my sisters maybe would play one of the current popular songs on the piano, and we'd sing. Or my mother or father would pick up a fiddle and begin playin', and we'd pick up the rugs and dance. Then we'd get somethin' to eat. But at ten o'clock they had to go home. That was the rule.

EDGEFIELD COUNTY, SOUTH CAROLINA, 1905

SOCIALS

A "social" is the name people gave to a community get-together that was held primarily for fun.

We always would select a moonlit night. We'd have chairs on the lawn and paper lanterns strung all over. And there'd be ice cream and cake you could buy for the benefit of the church. Maybe a hundred people would be there. The children would play games and run around. And the grown-ups would sit and talk—usually the men on one side of the lawn and the women on the other side. It might be ten-thirty or eleven o'clock before the last ones went home.

SAN ANTONIO, TEXAS, 1905

About once a month we'd get together and have singing and recitations and stunts and charades and things like that. One time we even had an "old folks" concert. People got dressed up in old-fashioned clothes and sang old-fashioned songs. At the end there'd be sandwiches and cake and coffee. Sometimes there'd be lobster. Everyone on the island would be there if they could. They would come on foot, carrying lanterns.

ISLE AU HAUT, MAINE, 1910

On a winter's night the whole family would pile into the sled and take some food along and go over to the schoolhouse for a spelling match. Everybody there would divide into two teams, and somebody would give the words—they'd be words like "rhythm" and "parallel" and "incinerate"—and we'd play until we had a winner. Then we'd eat and we'd socialize.

NEAR GREENE, IOWA, 1895

Three or four times a year we'd have a box supper at the schoolhouse. Mostly this was for the older kids. Each of the girls would fill a box with fried chicken, sandwiches, pickles, cookies, cake, things like that. Then they'd decorate the box so it looked really nice.

At the supper somebody would auction off each of the boxes for the benefit of the school. We weren't supposed to know whose supper we were biddin' on, but we certainly tried to figure it out. Because if you won you got to eat with the girl who fixed it. Actually, the bidding would go pretty high, as much as three or four dollars. But you got to meet some awfully nice girls that way.

JACKSON COUNTY, MISSOURI, 1910

PARTIES AND DANCES

When I was fifteen I went to my first party. It was at the neighbor's right over east of here. My brother and I went together. There were about twenty-five people there, all children our age. We played "Drop the Handkerchief" and "Ring Around the Rosie." And they had an organ, and we sang "Old Rugged Cross." And we had some popcorn and little cakes, and we drank water. Didn't know anything about soda pop then.

NEAR CLARKSVILLE, IOWA, 1895

Some nights we'd dance outside. We'd have two or three torches for light. And there'd be a banjo or a fiddle or somethin' like that. And we'd all go 'round in a ring clappin' our hands in time.

NEAR ALLISON, SOUTH CAROLINA, 1900

Somebody'd decide to have a square dance, and the word would come around, and everybody'd go. They'd just move all the furniture out of the living room, and the fiddlin' would start, and we'd dance.

EDGEWOOD, TEXAS, 1914

If you lived in one of the isolated Mormon settlements in Utah or Nevada, you could look forward to one dance a week, on a Friday night or a Saturday night.

The church sponsored it, and the whole community would go, whole families, some with babies. By the time I was fifteen or sixteen, I might go with a partner. Before that I went with my mother and father.

The way they had things arranged, the men and the boys would sit on one side of the church hall, and the women and girls would sit on the other side. To start, one of the older

111

men would stand and pray that we enjoy ourselves. Then the one who managed the dance would call out, "Fill up the floor for a waltz!" And the men and the boys would come across the hall to choose a partner.

You'd sit there wondering whether somebody was going to come and get you, and sometimes nobody did. But a boy would always dance with his mother, and a father would always dance with his daughters. And if you had a boyfriend, he would always dance with your sister. But he must not dance every dance with you. That was not allowed.

We had a piano for those dances, and sometimes we also would have a violin and a horn. Besides the waltz, we might do the two-step and the polka and the schottische, and the quadrille and other square dancing.

About halfway through, they might also have a mixer. We would go behind a curtain and stick our shoes out. The boys would get a number, and they would put their number on the shoe they thought a particular girl was wearing. Of course, sometimes we would switch shoes. So a boy wouldn't always get the girl he hoped he was getting. But whoever he got, he would share her lunch.

Usually the dance ended at twelve o'clock. Then one of the men would thank the Lord for the pleasure we had.

BUNKERVILLE, NEVADA, 1910

A schottische is a round dance something like a polka.

When I went to a dance in junior high school, a boy came to get me. Then my father went with us on the streetcar, and when it was over he'd come back for us. These dances usually were in somebody's living room. They would roll back the rugs and sprinkle wax powder on the floor to make it slippery. Then somebody would play the piano or the Victrola, and we would dance, and we would eat, and we would talk about school.

One time there was no place to sit. So this boy and I went out on the porch and sat in a swing. When my father came for us, he saw us out there. After we got home, he told me I must never again leave a party. And I must never go on a porch with a boy. It just wasn't done.

LOS ANGELES, 1910

If a girl was invited to a party, usually her hostess arranged for a boy to bring her and to take her home. That was his only responsibility for her. But she tried to pair off boys and girls who were interested in each other, or who might be. A Victrola was an early phonograph that transmitted sound through a large horn.

Most of the black sharecroppers on the plantations around Cade, Louisiana, belonged to the Golden Rule Society. The dues were twenty-five cents a month. If a member got sick or died, the society would help pay for the doctor or the funeral. The first Saturday of every month it also held a dance in a building in town.

My sister and I, oh, we would get all dressed up. We would wear our Sunday dresses and Sunday shoes and stockin's, and we'd fix our hair. Then we'd walk to the dance. It was two, three miles. My mommy and daddy and auntie would come with us, and they'd sit with the other mommies and daddies and watch. You see, we was big now—seventeen, eighteen— and we had to enjoy ourselves just like they enjoy themselves when they was young.

They would have a big band. It would be the violin and the guitar and the trombone and sometimes the accordion. We would do the quadrille and the one-step and the two-step and the waltz. If a boy wanted to dance with you, he wouldn't just say, "Let's go dance." He would come holdin' a white hand-kerchief and ask you in a serious way. Then he would fold his

113

handkerchief in his hand so he wouldn't touch your back, because that would not be proper.

Sometimes he would treat you. They have a table with some bananas, oranges, pralines, popcorn, things like that, and you would take what you want, and he would pay for that.

After the dance that boy or some other boy would walk home with us in the dark. When we got there, my mommy would say, *"Reviens."* "Come again." And I would say, *"Merci beaucoup."* "Thank you very much." Then he would go back to his house.

CADE, LOUISIANA, 1905

Cade is in a French-speaking section of Louisiana. It was common almost everywhere in this country for men and boys to wear white gloves at a dance so they wouldn't touch their partners with their bare hands. If you didn't have gloves, you held a folded white handkerchief in one hand as the young men in Cade did.

When our sorority had a dance, we would spend days fixing up the room. We would make paper flowers and hang them by threads from all over the ceiling. It was just elegant. And we'd push couches into the corners and put Navajo blankets and pillows on 'em. We called these "cozy corners." That's where you'd go with a boy and sit between dances. It was right out in the open, but you'd feel sort of wicked sitting there, just the two of you.

Usually some select [special] boy would ask me to go, and I'd get permission from my mother. Then he'd come to get me, and he'd be all done up, and I'd be all done up, and we'd go on the streetcar. When we got there, he got me a dance card with all the different dances listed. And he'd put himself down for the first and the last and one or two somewhere in the middle. Then other boys would come along and sign up for the rest.

TUCSON, ARIZONA, 1905

When we got a little older, they had these "play-parties" for us. Every week they'd have one, just to give us somethin' to do. But they wouldn't have any dancin' there or any fiddlin' or other music. The people here didn't believe in that.

NEAR SHANNON CITY, IOWA, 1905

In those days, many deeply religious people believed that dancing and playing the fiddle were evil. As a result, there were no dances in Shannon City and in many other places. Instead, young people went to play-parties where they played singing games, kissing games, and ordinary games, and often these were very lively affairs.

In the singing games, they would skip and march and swing their partners as they sang the words. Those who were not playing would clap their hands and tap their feet to the rhythm of the song. In a sense, the skipping, marching, and swinging were a kind of dancing, and the singing was a kind of music, but they didn't see it that way.

These singing games included "Go In and Out the Window," "Three Dukes," "London Bridge," and "Oats, Beans, Barley, and Rye." They were games that young children also played and sometimes still play. But with the large number of players, the lively, complicated movements, and the spirited singing and clapping, they were not quite the same.

Probably the most popular singing game in those years was "Skip to My Lou." "Lou" is a Tennessee term for sweetheart. One version of the song begins this way: "Flies in the buttermilk two by two, / Flies in the buttermilk shoo fly shoo, / Flies in the buttermilk two by two, / Skip to my Lou, my darling."

There are many verses, all of which follow the same pattern. One begins, "Little red wagon painted blue"; another, "Ma made buttermilk in Dad's old shoe;" another, "Pretty as a redbird, prettier too."

In this game the players form a circle. As they sing, a couple steps inside and chooses another boy to join them. The three hold hands and skip all the way around. Then the first boy and girl raise their arms and form an arch, and the new boy steps through. At this, the couple rejoins the circle, and he chooses another couple and they skip all the way around. Then he and the girl form an arch, and the other boy steps through. And so the game continues.

At Christmas, when everybody was home from school, we would go out into the country to this inn at East Eddington. We'd go with a team of horses in a pung [a sleigh with a box-shaped body], and the pung would be filled with hay and blankets. Altogether there'd be fifteen or twenty of us. We'd start out at maybe three o'clock in the afternoon and ride through the snow about twelve miles to this place. They'd have a roaring fire waiting for us and a good hot fish chowder. Then when we finished eating, they'd clear the dining room and we'd dance. At ten, eleven o'clock we'd start home, and we'd sing all the way.

BANGOR, MAINE, 1910

KISSING GAMES

Teenagers everywhere were playing kissing games then. It was one of the most popular activities at a party. A Vermont man said, "We wouldn't think we had a good evenin' unless we was kissed half to death."

"POST OFFICE"
One time at this party they put a girl in a bedroom and somebody stood at the door. He was the postmaster, and he said, "Charlie, got a letter for ya with two stamps." That meant two kisses. So I went in to get my letter, and the girl

116

—she was older than me and must have been kind of hot-blooded—well, she just grabbed me and was hugging the devil out of me, and I was wishing I could get out of there. Well, she finally got done. Then she was the postmaster, and I was the kisser.

INDIANAPOLIS, 1905

"WALK A CEDAR SWAMP"

A fella and a girl stood at opposite ends of the room, and she would ask him questions. Usually these were kind of personal questions, but he had to answer truly "yes" or "no." If he answered "no," he took one step toward her. If he answered "yes," he took one step away. When they got close enough to kiss, he could kiss her—if he could catch her.

WEST NEWBURY, VERMONT, 1890

"WINK"

There would be a circle of chairs, and a boy stood behind each one. And a girl sat in each one, except for one chair, which was empty. The boy who stood behind the empty chair tried to get one of the girls to change places and sit in it. He did this by winking at her. But if she tried to move, the boy behind her would try to grab her and keep her there. If he succeeded, he got to kiss her. But if she escaped, he was It and had to do the winking.

AUGUSTA, GEORGIA
LEXINGTON, KENTUCKY
1910–1914

"SPIN THE PAN"

We stood in a circle, and a boy stood in the center with a pie pan. He'd set the pan spinning and at the same time call out the name of a girl in the circle. Then she had to catch the pan before it stopped spinning. If she didn't, he would kiss her and set it spinning again. But if she caught it, it would be her turn to spin the pan.

DETROIT, 1910

"POSSUM PIE"

We stood in a circle—boy, girl, boy, girl—and held out both hands. Then somebody stood in the center and recited this rhyme:

> "Possum pie is made of rye,
> The possum is the meat,
> It's tough enough and rough enough,
> And more than we can eat."

For each word he recited he touched somebody's hand, going around and around the circle until he reached the end. If he touched your hand when he said "meat," you had to kiss the person he touched when he said "eat." You had to do it whether it was a girl or a boy. It didn't matter.

LYNCHBURG, VIRGINIA, 1900

My Birthday

People might say, "Happy birthday!" but that was all. It was just like any other day. There was no present and no party, and I didn't expect any. They didn't think much about such things.

OSAGE COUNTY, MISSOURI, 1890

When I was in fourth grade, I got a birthday card. A girl in school sent it to me. It was the latest thing.

JACKSON COUNTY, MISSOURI, 1908

The man fetched the card out of a box to show me. It looked like a picture postcard. On one side there were red flowers. On the other side there was a printed message and a place for the address. But the message wasn't as cheerful as those today. It read: "When the golden sun is setting, / And this earth you no more may trod, / May your name be written / In the autographs of God. / Happy birthday."

The first thing in the morning Mother would wish me a happy birthday, and we would embrace. Then she would say, "What kind of a meal should we make?" So I would decide what kind of soup, what kind of meat, and what kind of cake. Then we would make the meal together, and that night the whole family would eat it.

SEATTLE, 1910

Each year I had a birthday party for my friends, and we always had a Jack Horner Pie. This was a wash basin or something like that all covered with beautiful fringed tissue paper. Inside there was a gift for each child, and there was a long ribbon from the gift to where the child sat at the table. When my mother gave the signal, everybody pulled his ribbon, and the tissue paper broke and gifts flew through the air.

TUCSON, ARIZONA, 1895

How We Celebrated the Holidays

NEW YEAR'S DAY

Right at midnight the men all over town would fire their guns and pistols straight up into the sky. The locomotives in the freight yards would blow their whistles. The bells at the churches would ring out. And if you had firecrackers, you'd set them off.

TUCSON, ARIZONA, 1905

We would go from house to house and wish each other a happy new year. *"Une bonne année,"* we would say. *"Une bonne année,"* they would say. At every house we visited the table was set with food. My parents would have something to drink, and I would have some cake or something like that. At every house.

LAFAYETTE PARISH, LOUISIANA, 1905

Lafayette Parish was in a French-speaking section of Louisiana. Une bonne année means "a good year."

I would clasp my hands in front of me and say in Chinese, "I wish you a long life and happiness." My friends would do the same thing. Then we would sit and eat watermelon seeds and candies and drink sweet tea and talk about our future.

SAN FRANCISCO, CHINESE DISTRICT, 1905

We would celebrate by goin' to church. Then we would come home at twelve o'clock at night and cook black-eyed peas and collard greens. The peas was to get silver money in the new year. The collard greens was for greenbacks, paper money. Then we'd eat a little bit of each and say, "Happy new year!" Later on we'd see our friends and say, "Haven't seen you since last year."

AUGUSTA, GEORGIA, 1900

EASTER

Many children did not go hunting for Easter eggs. Instead, they would leave a small basket or box somewhere, and on Easter morning there would be half a dozen eggs in it and maybe some candy. Of course, now and then they'd find even more. One time a girl in New Orleans found a basket five feet long and about two feet wide filled with sugar rabbits, chocolate rabbits, toy rabbits, jelly beans, colored eggs, chocolate eggs, and spy eggs.

A spy egg was a hollow egg made of sugar. It had a hole at one end, and when you looked through the hole you saw a country scene or a city scene. When you got tired of doing that, you ate the egg—except for the scene, which was printed on paper.

Some people colored eggs with dyes they bought in a store, just as people do today. But many used natural dyes. To turn an egg green they boiled it with young blades of wheat. To color it yellow, they cooked it with the bark from a hickory tree. To color it a kind of brown, they cooked it with onion skins.

There was at least one game children played with their Easter eggs. It took two players. Each held an egg in one hand with the small end pointing out. Then they knocked the two ends together. The player whose egg cracked lost it to the other player. In Louisiana, French-speaking children called this game "Toc" after a French word for "to knock" or "to rap."

MAY DAY

In some places people celebrated by selecting a pretty young woman as May Queen. They would have a ceremony at which she was crowned, and there'd be a picnic. In other places young people made May baskets and gave them to persons they especially liked.

I'd take a small cardboard box and put a handle on it, and I'd decorate it with flowers and fill it with fruit and candy. Then around dark, a few of us would go out together to deliver our boxes and baskets.

Usually I'd leave mine with some girl I thought was nice. I'd put it on her doorstep and rap on the door, and we'd all run. Then she'd have to come out and find us. Of course, we wouldn't try very hard to hide. But if she found me first, I might get to kiss her. That's what I hoped. Anyway, when she found us all, we'd go back to the house and talk and fool around and get somethin' to eat. Then we'd go on to the next stop.

MARTHA'S VINEYARD, MASSACHUSETTS, 1900

It was the rule that each person who was caught had to help catch the others. Traditionally May Day was observed on May 1. But some young people would deliver a different May basket night after night until they couldn't afford any more fruit or candy.

DECORATION DAY

This was a day when the graves of men who died in the Civil War were decorated. Often the schoolchildren in a town would march to the local cemetery carrying flowers, then place the flowers on the graves. Usually there also would be a program at the school. In the North, this holiday was observed on May 30. In the South, it was observed on various other days.

There would be maybe half a dozen Civil War veterans there. And there'd be some pupils who recited verses like "The Flag Is Passing By" and how they're all dead, and here's the Grey and here's the Blue, and all of 'em are in the same cemetery now, or somethin' like that.

Then I had a friend who would recite "Morgan, Morgan, the raider." Each verse ended up, "Morgan, Morgan, the terrible raider, and Morgan's terrible men." It tells the story about a woman who's alone at home on the farm, and she hears that Morgan's men are coming—they were cavalrymen and they were picking up horses where they could—and how she hid her fine horse Belle, Kentucky Belle, in the cornfield or somewhere. And Morgan's men

124

stopped and looked and couldn't find anything and finally galloped on away. And when they left she still had Belle, safe and sound.

Then the principal would have one of us make a speech. He wrote it and we memorized it. It always started out, "Members of the Grand Army [of the] Republic, we are glad to welcome you here today. . . ."

Then each of the old soldiers would tell us what he remembered about the war. One of them told us about one place where they got beat and they had to just run to get away. "And the only reason I was runnin'," he said, "was because I couldn't fly."

SALEM, OREGON, 1910

After World War I, Decoration Day became known as Memorial Day, when the dead of all wars are honored. "Morgan, Morgan, the terrible raider" was General John H. Morgan, a Confederate scout who became famous for his daring raids on Union positions in Kentucky, Ohio, and Indiana.

THE FOURTH OF JULY

Early in the morning, about four o'clock, they'd fire the anvils. These would be anvils the blacksmith used. They'd have a square hole at one end, and they'd put one anvil on the ground and fill that hole with black gunpowder. Then they'd take the other anvil and put it on top so that the holes matched, and they filled that hole with gunpowder. Then they'd put a long fuse up there, and they'd light it. When it exploded it was like a cannon going off. And the anvil on top flew up into the sky. That was the beginning of the Fourth of July.

ORDERVILLE, UTAH, 1900

Why, people would come ten miles with their wagons, and maybe they'd come the day before and pick a shady spot along the creek to spend the night. Everybody'd bring stuff out of their gardens and stuff out of their kitchens. And they'd bring their best pies and their best cakes. And they'd have their ice cream freezers with 'em, and plenty of cream and salt.

In the morning somebody'd go to town to get ice and lemons and whatever else we needed. And when he got back they'd start in crankin' the freezers. And they'd get out a barrel and cut the lemons and squeeze 'em out with one of those little old squeezers, and throw the hulls and everything in there, and some sugar and water and ice. And my dad, he'd call out:

> "Lemonade—
> Made in the shade,
> Stirred with a spade!"

And we kids would go 'round suckin' them lemons, eat 'em rinds and all.

Then nearly always somebody had some horses that could buck, and they'd get these horses to buckin'. And, oh, there'd be buckin' contests and horse races and burro races and sack races and three-legged races and women's races and men's races and kids' races and other races.

Then at night after supper the kids would speak pieces, and everybody'd sing songs, mostly every kind of song that was ever invented, I guess.

OAK CREEK, ARIZONA, 1910

In a lot of places there would be a parade and maybe a baseball game with a team from another town, and at night there might be a dance. In some sections of the South, people ignored the Fourth. They regarded it as a Yankee holiday. But in others they'd have big public picnics that a thousand people might attend. And, of course, almost everywhere, there were firecrackers going off.

We had little firecrackers called Baby Wakers. And we had Torpedoes. They were about two, three inches long, and you'd throw 'em against a wall or a rock. Then we had them big cannon crackers, five, six inches long, a couple of inches around. They was just wicked. You'd put a hat over one, light it—and that hat would be gone, just blown all to pieces. A lot of times kids lost a hand foolin' around with them. Just blowed their fingers right off.

COMO, COLORADO, 1895

Every year Father would buy us a case of firecrackers. Then about five o'clock in the morning we would get up and go out into the street, and he would sit out on the front steps and watch, and we would shoot them off. But by seven o'clock we'd be tired of it. So we would put what was left in a big pile and set it all off together, with one big bang.

Didn't the neighbors complain?

Everybody was doing it.

NEW YORK, UPPER EAST SIDE DISTRICT, 1895

HALLOWE'EN

For weeks the neighbors saved any wood they had. Then after supper we had this big bonfire in the street, and we'd leap and jump and dance around it like witches.

BROOKLYN, NEW YORK, 1900

All of us would carve a squash or a pumpkin into a jack-o'-lantern and put a candle in it. After it got dark we'd go around to different houses and rap on the window and hold our jack-o'-lanterns up so that they could see them. Then they'd

127

come to the door and chase us for a while. That was the custom.

DEER ISLE, MAINE, 1900

We'd take these old sheets and cut eyes in them, and we'd get some soot and make black rings around the eyes. Then we'd fix up some ears like Satan's, cut them out of an old black hat or somethin', and we'd pin them on. Then we'd put on our sheets and go down to the tenant houses [where workers on this plantation lived], just hootin' and hollerin' and makin' an awful racket. When they heard us, why, they'd grab up their sheets and come along. From house to house we'd go, scaring everybody we could.

FRANKLIN COUNTY, GEORGIA, 1895

In those days that was the whole idea of Hallow-e'en: to scare somebody or to startle them or perhaps annoy them. A tick tack was standard equipment.

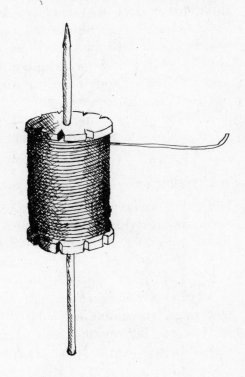

To fix up a tick tack, you would take an empty thread spool, cut notches in the ends, and wrap a string around the middle. Then you would put a stick through the spool so it had something to spin on.

To use it, you would sneak up to somebody's window. Then with one hand you would hold the stick so that the spool pressed against the glass. With the other hand, you would jerk the string. When the spool started spinning against that glass, it made an awful noise, sort of a screeching sound. Old man Brock used to jump out of his chair whenever I did that to him.

BETHANY, NEBRASKA, 1905

To make a tick tack you will need a wooden thread spool. A plastic one won't work.

We'd go up to somebody's front door and tie one end of a rope to their doorknob and the other end to the porch railing or a tree. Then we'd bang on the door and run. When they came to open it, well—they couldn't.

HELENA, MONTANA, 1910

All day we'd sneak up behind people, and we'd hit them with a sock full of flour or we'd mark up their clothes with chalk. At night we'd ring doorbells. We'd stick a pin in a bell so that it would keep ringing, then we'd run. But if you weren't fast enough, they'd open the door, and you might get a dish of water in your face.

BROOKLYN, NEW YORK, 1900

Some older boys weren't so peaceful. They tipped over outhouses, hung fences from telephone poles, hoisted buggies up on barn roofs,

129

and locked cows in schoolhouses, among other pranks. One time in Boulder, Montana, they built a solid wall of stovewood during the night. It was six feet high and went all the way across Main Street. In New Orleans there were boys who celebrated the holiday with "gutter water." The city had gutters next to the sidewalks to carry off rainwater, and the bottoms of these gutters were covered with a slimy muck. "They would fill paper bags with this stuff," a woman remembered. "And if they caught you, they'd break them over your head. Then—eeeeeeeeeeeeeh!"

THANKSGIVING

Each year we went to Grandfather's brother's house for Thanksgiving. We always had turkey, escalloped potatoes, mashed potatoes, sweet potatoes, creamed onions, cranberries, and all the rest. One Thanksgiving there were thirty-five people at that table, and two turkeys. Mother carved at one end, and one of the relatives carved at the other end. They had a race, and Mother won.

INDEPENDENCE, MISSOURI, 1900

Thanksgiving night there was the Thanksgiving masquerade ball. That was a regular feature here. Everybody went. People would get dressed up as clowns and princesses and kings and devils and everything. There was a costumer who came up on the train from Denver with all the costumes. He'd stay at the rooming house in town, and you could go over there and rent a costume from him for a dollar. Nobody knew for sure who anybody was until after midnight. Then we took off our masks, and we had a good lunch, and we danced some more.

COMO, COLORADO, 1895

Como was an isolated railroad junction in the Rocky Mountains about ninety miles from Denver, or about four hours by train. Only a few hundred people lived there.

CHRISTMAS

We'd look in the woods for a tree. When we found one we liked, we'd cut it and load it on our sledge and bring it home, trailing it behind us through the deep snow.

NEAR WAUKEGAN, ILLINOIS, 1910

The night before Christmas we made paper chains and lovely large loops of popcorn and hung them on the tree. And Mother baked butter cookies and made a hole in each with a pin, and ran a string through the hole, and hung them on the tree. And we'd polish up some apples and oranges and put them on.

When all that was done, my dad would put on the candle-holders and the candles. Then very carefully he would light them. All of us would stand there for five, ten minutes not saying anything, just watching this beautiful, glowing, flickering tree. Then finally he would blow them out.

DETROIT, 1910

Many people decorated their trees with candles, but nobody burned them for very long, for they could easily set a tree on fire. (As a precaution, a bucket of sand or water usually was kept nearby.) Because oranges were costly, Christmas was the only time many families had them. Usually they served as both decorations and gifts. To hang an orange from a tree, you put it in a small net, then attached the net to a sturdy branch.

In rural areas many people did not have a Christmas tree at home. Either it was not the custom, or trees were hard to obtain or were too costly. Instead there might be a community tree at a church or a schoolhouse. It would be there that the community had its Christmas party.

Everybody in town would be at that party. Each kid would get a bag of candy. It was hardtack, sort of like candy cane. And the town orchestra would play, and we'd dance. "Sally Waters" was the main dance. Your partner would face you and you'd hold hands, and it was left foot, right foot, any foot at all. Then you'd go hoppin' along three or four steps. Then you'd do it over again.

Somewhere in the middle Santa Claus would come in with his wife. He would have on his regular Santa Claus suit, and she'd be wearing just ordinary clothes with a shawl over her head. Actually she was a man, and the first thing, she would walk on her hands. Then Santa Claus would get up by the tree and hand out the presents. If somebody wanted to give you a gift, they'd hang it on the tree. So everybody always got quite a few.

BEAR RIVER CITY, UTAH, 1900

"Little Sally Waters" was both a game and a dance. A girl sits in the center of a ring of players from whom she chooses the boy she loves "best." After he joins her, the other players dance around them, singing of courtship and marriage. In one version they give the boy, by then a "husband," some advice: "Now you are married / You must be good / And help your wife / To chop the wood. / Chop it thin / And bring it in / And kiss her over / And over again."

We'd hang our stockin's by the fireplace, and we'd sit in the front room and wait for him. Poppa would tell us, "Santa is comin'. You all better behave."

Then about eight o'clock or so he'd walk in. When we saw him, of course we was all kind of shaky. He had a sheet wrapped around him and a little gray hat sittin' on top of his head, kind of a lavender color, and some old gray whiskers put all over his face. He looked sort of like a ghost.

He'd ask us, "You all been good?"

And we'd tell him, "Yeah."

Then he'd put somethin' in each of the stockin's, and he'd say to Poppa, "How are the children?"

And Poppa said, "Well, sometimes they're pretty good, and sometimes they're pretty bad."

Then he'd look at us again and he'd say, "If you don't be good, I'm comin' back [and take your presents away]."

Actually he was our uncle, but we didn't know it.

NEW ORLEANS, 1890

Right after my father died, my uncle told my mother that he was going to bring us our Christmas. Well, back in them days and times, around Christmas they kept the stores open till twelve o'clock at night. And he finished up his shoppin' pretty late, and he had to get in a buggy and drive down here, and that took him an hour or more. It was so late when he arrived, he was afraid he'd wake us all up. So he put a big box on the front porch.

The next mornin' my mother got up before we did, and she began runnin' around lookin' to see what had happened and why her brother hadn't brought the stuff to her. And finally she found this box on the front porch. And there were apples and oranges in it, and all candies and stuff, and a lot of toys.

Well, we always thought Santa Claus come down the chimney, and we had our stockin's hanging up there, and there was nothin' in 'em, and, of course, we were badly disappointed. So Mother told us, "You remember we stayed up late last night, and we had a big fire. The chimney got so hot, Santa Claus couldn't come down. So he left the stuff on the front porch." And she took us out there and showed it to us, and we just like to have a fit.

MILFORD, GEORGIA, 1900

They always said Santy Claus brought all that stuff. So one year I waited up so I could get a look at him. While I was waitin', I saw my mother and my daddy fillin' the stockin's. So I called out, "Hell, there ain't no Santy Claus."

And my daddy says, "You need a whuppin'."

And I says, "But you ain't gonna give it to me. You been tellin' stories."

CARROLL COUNTY, GEORGIA, 1905

This boy and this girl dressed up something like Joseph and Mary, and they went from house to house looking for a place where Jesus could be born, and a crowd followed them. They knocked on every door, and if somebody answered they sang one verse of this very long song. [Each verse tells part of the Christmas story as it unfolds.]

"In the name of heaven," the boy sang, "I ask you for a place to stay because the Virgin is tired and worn out." That was the first verse, and the crowd sang with him. But at each place they tried, the people turned them away.

Finally they came to a manger set up at somebody's house and the search was over, and there was a party. There was food and something to drink, and hanging up high there was a big clay *piñata* filled with candy. The two were blindfolded, and with sticks they reached up and tried to break it. When they did, everybody dove for the candy.

BROWNSVILLE, TEXAS, 1910

134

This Mexican ceremony is called "Las Posadas." In Spanish it means "lodgings." It reenacts the Christmas story and is repeated each night on the seven nights before Christmas. When Mexican families began to move north into Texas, Arizona, and New Mexico, they brought this tradition with them.

We Go to Church

Saturday nights the ranch hands and the prospectors would come to town for some fun, and usually they'd get drunk. Well, Sunday morning on the way to Sunday School, we'd find them sleepin' all over the sidewalk. So we'd get a runnin' start and jump over 'em, then look back to see if we woke 'em up. Then we'd go on to church.

BOULDER, MONTANA, 1910

Since Father was a minister, we had to get up early on Sunday mornings. First thing, he'd make pancakes for us. Then he'd go into the parlor and close the door and practice

136

his sermon. He might be there two hours walking up and down talking out loud to himself.

When we got to church, we all helped. One of my brothers pumped the organ and Mother played, and the rest of us sang in the choir. Father preached his sermon without a single note. He just stood up there and told them what was in his mind. But when we got back home, he was so worn out he'd fall asleep in the rocking chair. And while he slept, we got dinner ready.

CHICO, CALIFORNIA, 1910

We'd get dressed up, and take our dinner with us, and go to church in the wagon—and we'd stay all day. It was for religion, of course. But it was a gathering time, too.

The preacher would begin by reading one line out of the Bible and telling what it meant. Then he'd read the next line and explain that. He'd go through a whole passage that way. Then he'd preach this sermon about what would happen if you didn't do good, how hellfire and damnation were waitin' for you. And you had a feeling he knew just what he was talkin' about.

When he got through, he'd ask if there was anybody who was ready to join the church. That meant repenting your sins and giving up your life to Jesus. Then maybe some man might stand up and say, "I've done some awful things, and I want the Lord to forgive me." And he'd tell what he had done, confess everything right in front of his neighbors and everybody. The preacher would put his hand on that man's head and he'd pray for him and ask him if he was ready to start a new life and be born again. And he'd say, "Yes, I want to dedicate my life to Jesus." It was a very serious thing for him, and people would call out encouragement and sing and cry.

Well, then we'd eat. Everybody brought whatever food he wanted, and it all would be put on one table, and you'd go and

137

help yourself. Mother would put a tablecloth on the ground under a tree, and we'd sit around that, and the others did the same.

After the food, the elders would talk and the children would play. Then they would hold singings, what they called Sacred Harp singings. The preacher would have a little pitch pipe and he'd sound it to set the pattern. Then everybody'd sing.

EDGEWOOD, TEXAS, 1910

This was a Southern Baptist service. The Sacred Harp hymns traditionally are sung without accompaniment and have a range of four notes rather than the usual eight. This makes them easier to sing. Probably the best known of these hymns is "Amazing Grace."

My parents belonged to the Salvation Army. My father played a snare drum in the Army band. And my mother went around to the saloons selling their newspaper—*The War Cry,* it was called—and urging people not to drink.

On Sunday mornings they'd get into their uniforms, and we'd go to church at the Salvation Army Hall. Then we'd all march downtown with the band playing and have a public meeting in some park to get new members. Then we'd march back to the hall for the evening service. People stared at us like we were peculiar, and the kids called after us. After a while, I wouldn't go anymore. It was too embarrassing.

CAMBRIDGE, MASSACHUSETTS, 1905

Sunday School was at ten o'clock. We sang hymns and they read us Bible stories and we memorized Bible verses. They'd give each of us a little card that had a verse on it and a picture of some innocent-looking child or somethin'. When you could recite that verse, you'd get another card. And when you got five of them, you'd get a big one to keep. So we spent quite

138

a bit of time on that. Then toward the end of the morning they passed the collection plate. We would drop our pennies in and sing:

> "Dropping, dropping, dropping, dropping,
> Hear the pennies fall,
> Every one for Jesus,
> He can use them all."

ATLANTA, 1910

The day I was baptized I wore a white gown my mother made for me. The whole church went down to this pond in the woods. The preacher led the way, and we marched right through town singing hymns. When we got there, he took off his shoes and walked out into the water, and I took off mine and followed him.

Then he put his hand on my head, and he said, "I now baptize you in the name of the Father, the Son, and the Holy Ghost." And he carried me straight down into the water, all the way down, and brought me back up, and took a towel and wiped my face.

Then two of the women took me on home and got the wet clothes off me. And I got all dressed up, and we went back to the church and had Communion and fellowship. I was only twelve years old, but I felt like a grown-up.

AUGUSTA, GEORGIA, 1899

After church we would have a chicken dinner. Then the elders would take a nap. Later we would play the piano and sing hymns, but we couldn't play games. It wasn't allowed. If it was a nice day we would walk over the farm to see if the fences were all right and how the crops were growing. Just kind of watch, you know.

We would wear our church clothes all day. So did our

139

father, except for feeding the animals. Sometimes the minister would come for dinner, and that would be something. Or sometimes we would go to my grandmother's to eat. In the evenings we would talk a good deal. Often Father would tell us about his boyhood time, and Mother would tell us about when she was young.

NEAR WAUKEGAN, ILLINOIS, 1905

Other Things We Believed

No grass grew in our yard, but there were doodlebugs there. I'd take a can and a string and try to catch them. I'd drop the string down a doodlebug hole and say:

"Doodlebug, doodlebug, come get some corn,
Your house is on fire and your children will burn."

If I said that, there'd always be one hanging on. That's what I believed. Then I'd pull up the string and put the ones I caught in the can. When I finished, I'd put them back in their holes so there'd be some the next time.

SWANSBORO, NORTH CAROLINA, 1910

In some places children didn't use string. They just put their mouths close to the hole and hollered for the doodlebug to come out until he did. Since doodlebugs eat ants, they are also called ant lions.

My father said, "If you put a horsehair in a jar of water it will turn into a snake."

My mother said, "If you start something on Friday, and if you don't finish it that day, you never will."

My grandma said, "Don't sweep the doorstep on New Year's Eve. You'll sweep your friends away."

I had this friend and he said, "When you walk into a building, walk out the same door or you'll have bad luck."

STOCKTON, CALIFORNIA
CHARLESTON, SOUTH CAROLINA
DETROIT
BEDFORD COUNTY, TENNESSEE
1890–1910

For good luck, some people made a hole in a dime and wore it around their ankle. And some hung a dried rabbit's foot from their neck. Some also wore an alligator tooth, but that was to protect against toothache.

AUGUSTA, GEORGIA
NEW ORLEANS
1890–1900

Now and then I would see a ball of fire flyin' just above the trees. It always had a short tail on it, and the tail shook. Wherever that ball of fire would bust, somebody would die.

PENOBSCOT INDIAN VILLAGE, INDIAN ISLAND, MAINE, 1910

Mama believed in spirits. A spirit is something that comes back from the dead and you can see it, just like you can see a real person. Well, one night she said that Poppa's mother was walkin' around the room with a shawl on. We couldn't see nothin'. But she says to her, "Hello, Mother, how are ya?" Oh, we was scared.

AUGUSTA, GEORGIA, 1895

After Supper

We would help Mother clean up, and when we were finished with that we'd do our schoolwork at the kitchen table. Then we might get a basin of apples from the cellar and maybe some crackers from the cupboard. My mother and father would sit near the stove, and my sister and I would lie on the floor. And we'd eat apples and crackers and talk about things.

PATTEN, MAINE, 1910

Sometimes Daddy would read to us from the paper or the Bible. I thought he was just awful to do that. And sometimes we'd have games around the fire. And sometimes we'd sing. We sang religious songs and funny songs and what we called "love songs," just a lot of those. I would sit in my father's lap, and he would teach me the notes. In the wintertime we also popped corn a good deal.

BEDFORD COUNTY, TENNESSEE, 1890

Some nights Father would bring out his accordion. Then everybody would go into the kitchen—that was the biggest room—and he'd teach us dances from the old country. We would all get into a circle, all seven of us, and he'd play his accordion, and we'd go hoppin' around—first this way, then that way. . . .

DETROIT, 1910

At night my mother and father and the neighbors would sit on the front steps and talk. We kids would sit with 'em and listen. After a while they'd send us down to the saloon on the corner for some beer. We'd take this quart bucket with us and go in the side door and for a dime he'd fill it up. Then they'd pass the bucket from one to the other and when it was empty they'd send us back for more.

NEW YORK, HELL'S KITCHEN DISTRICT, 1900

When we got big enough to stay out after dark, we hung around the drugstore and almost aggravated the owner to death. We'd stand out front, fool around, make a racket, block the door. When we got tired of that, we'd get under the streetlight and throw pebbles at the bats. And when we got tired of that, we'd play "Black Man"—try to get across the street in the dark without bein' caught. Then we'd go home.

ATLANTA, 1905

The rules for playing Black Man are on page 77.

Every night I had to go to sleep at eight o'clock. But first I would kneel and in Swedish I would say this prayer:

> *"Gud som haver barnen kär,*
> *Se till mig som liten är.*
> *Vart jag mig i världen vänder,*
> *Står min lycka i Guds händer."*

Then I would get into bed.

ONAWAY, MICHIGAN, 1900

The woman who remembered this prayer could not tell me exactly what it meant in English. Mary A. Chase of South Brooksville, Maine, translated it into these words:

> *"God who loves children,*
> *Look after me who is small.*
> *Wherever in the world I turn,*
> *My well-being is in God's hands."*

Tales They Told

I asked the people I visited to tell me the stories they were told when they were young. Some were traditional tales passed down from generation to generation over hundreds of years. The brief story of the soup stone in the chapter on peddlers was one of these. The story called "The Light" in this chapter was another. But most of their tales were family stories about experiences mothers and fathers and other relatives had had. These were the ones they remembered best.

"MY FATHER AND THE CATTLE RUSTLER"

Somebody was cuttin' the fences on my father's ranch and stealin' his cattle. Father was pretty sure who was doin' it. So he went into town lookin' for him. The first place he went was the saloon. He always said that if you wanted to find a man that was the place to start. And that's where this fella was.

So he went up to him and he said, "Pete, you've been stealin' my cattle."

And Pete said, "I have not! I have not!"

Well, they argued about it a little, and finally Father said, "No question about it. I know you've been stealin' them. I've got proof on ya and everything. If you come on my ranch and steal my cattle again, I'm goin' to kill ya." And he walked out.

Not too long after, this fella came back and stole another herd. And Father came on the tracks, and he took some of his men, and they found him, and there he was with the cattle. So Father went up to him and he said, "I told ya if I ever caught ya stealin' my cattle again, I'd kill ya."

And Pete fell to his knees and he said, "Oh, Joe, don't kill me! Don't kill me!"

And Father's men said, "Shoot him, Joe! Shoot him! You told him you would."

Well, Father was quiet for a minute. Then he said, "Pete, I never did shoot a man, and I never want to. But I'll tell ya what I'll do. I'll let you go if you promise me you'll get out of the country, and I mean today."

And, oh, he promised. He was scared to death, and he got out fast. And Father, he got his cattle back.

NEAR UVALDE, TEXAS, 1900

"HOW OKRA GOT INTO AMERICA"

Aunt Hester came over here on a slave ship. When she landed, Mr. Middleton bought her. He had the Middleton Plantations, and he gave her to his caretaker as a wife. She was only thirteen then. But when I knew her she was very old, and her hair was snow white.

She said that before she left her home in Africa, the slave trader gave her a sack. And he told her to go through the okra fields and fill it up with okra because that would be partly her food and partly her bed all the way over.

So with the others she came, each with a sack of okra. It took a month to cross, and when they got hungry they ate raw okra, and when they got tired they slept on their sacks with the okra inside.

By the time they got here, a lot of that okra had hardened into pods, and it was planted for a crop. That was how okra got into America.

CHARLESTON, SOUTH CAROLINA, 1905

Okra is a vegetable native to Africa.

"THE LIGHT"

It was in the wintertime, and this man and his wife were out in the woods campin'. That night he went out to look around, and he saw this light comin' from back of a tree, just as if somebody was watching them. So he got nervous, and he told his wife, "We'll leave tomorrow."

Well, they had a long way to go, and they were only travelin' by snowshoe, that and a sled he hauled with their stuff on it. So early the next morning they packed up and started off. But when night come, they looked back and there was that light. So they decided to keep goin'.

149

They just kept travelin' and travelin'. And when his wife got tired, she'd sit on the sled and he'd haul her for a while. But the light kept followin' them and gettin' closer and closer. After a while it got close enough so he could make out what it was.

It was a skeleton, and the light was where the heart used to be. Well, he got out his gun and started firin' at it, but the bullets didn't do any good. And it kept gettin' closer, and he didn't know what to do. After a while, he picked up a good long stick and put a sharp point on it. Then when that skeleton got close enough, he threw it right at the light. And the skeleton disappeared.

When he got home, he found that his father had died. That skeleton was his warning.

PENOBSCOT INDIAN VILLAGE, INDIAN ISLAND, MAINE, 1910

This tale suggests several traditional motifs in folk literature: E 363.3, "Ghost warns the living"; E 765, "Life bound up with light"; E 422.1.11.4, "Revenant as skeleton." The references are from Stith Thompson, Motif-Index of Folk-Literature.

"FANCY DIVING"

When he was fourteen years old this uncle of mine walked across the Great Plains to California. He came looking for gold, and he didn't find any. But he was a fine swimmer, so he went down to the waterfront and started diving for coins. People would toss them in, and he'd dive down and find them and keep them.

Then he started doing really fancy diving. For a poke of gold, he'd dive off the top of the pilothouse of a steamboat. And on his way down he'd turn a full gainer, stick his feet in the lifeboat, then just barely miss the guardrail. The guardrail was always the biggest thrill. One time he came so close to it,

150

it burned his stomach and his chin. He did real well, made quite a lot of money. But he drank it all up.

STOCKTON, CALIFORNIA, 1910

Walking to California, as this man's uncle did, was unusual. The few people who did this usually traveled in small groups. They also might have oxen with them to help carry their possessions. A poke of gold is a quarter of an ounce in a little sack.

"THE QUEEN OF IRELAND"

Grandma would say, "Would you like to hear about the time I was the queen of Ireland?" And we would say, "Oh, yes!" and we'd sit at her feet and listen.

But first she would tell us how green it is in Ireland, and how loving the Irish people are, and what a good man Saint Patrick was. And then she would tell us about the leprechauns —how the only people who can see them are Irish, and how a leprechaun will give you a pot of gold if you catch it and set it free. Then she would call us to the back [window] pane and show us one. Of course, if you already knew it was there, it wasn't too hard to see.

Finally, she would get to the part about being queen. She lived in this grand house and had all these servants and all the people loved her. But then there was this terrible famine, and there was nothing to eat in the whole country. So a great many people escaped into America, and she was one of them.

But if any soldiers ever came around and asked about her, we were never to tell where she was. If they found her, they would make her go back and be the queen again, and she didn't want to leave us. That was the source of her worry. When we got older we learned that she had never been to Ireland, but that didn't matter.

NEW ORLEANS, 1910

151

"UNCLE SAM FIGHTS A BEAR"

Uncle Sam Woods was hunting on horseback up on Powder Horn Ridge with a man by the name of Guy Guthrie. Now Powder Horn Ridge is way up above Pine Flat, just over the Sierra Divide.

When they set off hunting that morning, each man went in a different direction around the mountain. After a while, Uncle Sam came across this young black bear with a beautiful sheen to its fur. Since he hadn't killed any deer, he decided to settle for some bear meat. So he raised his gun and fired at the bear and wounded it.

But the shot startled his horse, and it reared up and threw him off. He went one way, and his gun went the other, and at the same time the bear attacked.

He pulled out his hunting knife and struggled with it for a while, but he was getting the worst of it. So he broke off and ran for this creek and jumped in, thinking maybe the bear couldn't swim. But it came right after him, and when he scrambled to get away he fell and lost his knife. So he caught hold of an overhanging tree limb and climbed up and hung on.

Meanwhile, that bear was growling and roaring and leaping up out of the water at him. So he decided his only chance was to jump him and try to drown him. And that's what he did, and he got a good hold around his neck. But the bear dragged him up out of the water and onto the bank and clawed his legs, and, when he got them clear, bit him on the buttocks.

Then somehow they got close to where that gun was lying. And when the bear lunged at him again, Uncle Sam grabbed it and shot him and killed him. But he was so badly clawed and mauled, he just lay there next to the bear.

He would have died had not Guy Guthrie heard the shots

and come to him and taken him to a hospital, hanging on face down across the back of his horse.

STOCKTON, CALIFORNIA, 1910

The man who told me this story first heard it when he was a boy. But he didn't know how it came out, because while Uncle Sam was telling it to him the dinner bell rang, and after dinner Uncle Sam forgot about this story and went on to another. After we had talked, the man got the rest of the story from his uncle's son and sent it on to me.

Songs We Sang

Almost everybody I talked to remembered singing at home with their parents. Many remembered the songs they sang. And some sat back and sang them. They were religious songs, folk songs, and what then were popular songs. The words and music for seven of these are given below just as they were sung. Professor Nahoma Sachs transcribed them from tape recordings made during my visits. She is a folklorist and an ethnomusicologist at Princeton University.

"I CAN BE STILL"

I can be still as any mouse,
There is a baby in our house,
Not a dolly, not a toy,
But a laughing, crying boy.

Rockabye baby on the treetop,
When the wind blows the cradle will rock,
When the bough breaks, the cradle will fall,
Down will come rockabye baby—and all.

NEAR GREENE, IOWA, 1890

"FROM WIDDLETON TO WADDLETON"

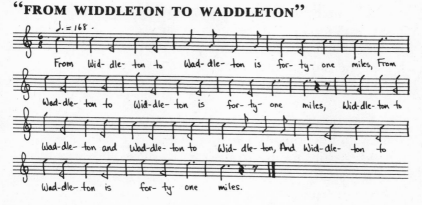

From Widdleton to Waddleton is forty-one miles,
From Waddleton to Widdleton is forty-one miles,
Widdleton to Waddleton and Waddleton to Widdleton,
And Widdleton to Waddleton is forty-one miles.

NEAR SHANNON CITY, IOWA, 1900

"BRAVE BOYS"

It was eighteen hundred and thirty-nine,
On the fourteenth day of May,
We weighed our anchor and set our sail,
And for Greenland bore away, brave boys,
And for Greenland bore away.

Now the captain's name it was William Moore,
And the mate's name was the same,
And the ship she was called the *Lion* so bold
As she plowed the raging main, brave boys,
As she plowed the raging main.

Now the captain he stood in the top crosstree,
And a fine-lookin' man was he,
A-searchin' the horizon with a spyglass in his hand,
"It's a whale, a whale, a fish, brave boys,
It's a whale, a fish!" cried he.

And the mate he stood on the quarterdeck,
And a fine-lookin' man was he.
"Overhaul, overhaul, at your davit tackle falls,
And just lower your boats to the sea, brave boys,
Just lower your boats to the sea."

Now the boats being lowered and the whale being struck,
He give one flurry with his tail,
And down went the boat and those six jolly tars,
And they never came up no more, brave boys,
No, they never came up no more.

When the captain heard of the loss of his men,
It grieved his heart full sore.
But when he heard of the loss of that whale,
Why it grieved him ten times more, brave boys,
Yes, it grieved him ten times more.

But the summer months are past and gone,
Cold winter is a-comin' on.
So we'll steer our course back to New Bedford,
And the pretty girls standin' on the shore, brave boys,
And the pretty girls standin' on the shore.

MARTHA'S VINEYARD, MASSACHUSETTS, 1895

This is a chantey, a song sailors sang while they worked. Usually it was sung without accompaniment. The man who told me about it no longer was able to sing it, so his son-in-law sang it for the tape recorder. It is better known as "The Greenland Whale" and "The Greenland Whalefishery." There are many versions of it. The "davit tackle" in the fourth verse is equipment that supports, raises, and lowers lifeboats and whaleboats. In Native American Balladry *by G. Malcolm Laws, the song is classified as K21.*

157

"THE TENDERFOOT"

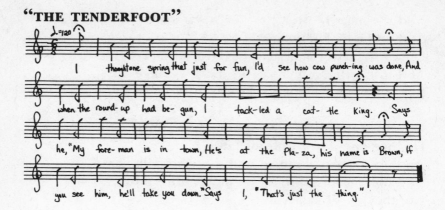

I thought one spring that just for fun,
I'd see how cowpunching was done,
And when the roundup had begun,
I tackled a cattle king.
Says he, "My foreman is in town,
He's at the Plaza, his name is Brown,
If you see him, he'll take you down."
Says I, "That's just the thing."

We started for the ranch next day,
Brown ordered me almost all the way,
Says cowpunching was nothing but play,
There was nothing to do at all.
That all you had to do was ride,
Just simply driftin' with the tide,
The son of a gun, oh, how he lied!
Don't you think he had his gall?

They put me in charge of the cow yard,
And they told me not to work too hard,
That all I had to do was guard

The cattle from gettin' away.
I had a hundred and fifty head,
Sometimes I wished that I was dead,
And one got away—Brown's hair turned gray,
And there was the devil to pay.

Sometimes a cow would make a break,
Across the mesa he would take,
As if he were a-runnin' for a stake,
To them it seemed but play.
Sometimes I couldn't stop 'em at all,
Sometimes my horse would catch a fall,
And I'd shoot on like a cannonball
Until the earth come in my way.

They saddled me up an old gray hack,
With two setfasts upon his back,
They padded him down with a gunny sack,
They used no beddin' at all.
When I got on he quit the ground,
Went up in the air and turned around,
When I come down, I busted the ground,
I got one terrible fall.

They picked me up, they packed me in,
They rolled me out with a bottle of gin,
And that's the way they all begin,
Says Brown, "You're doin' fine.
And in the mornin', if you don't die,
We'll give you another horse to try."
"Oh, no," says I, "I'd rather walk."
Says he, "Walk back to town."

I've traveled up, I've traveled down,
I've traveled this country 'round and 'round,
I've lived in the city, I've lived in town,
I've got this much to say.
When you try cowpunchin', kiss your wife,
Take a heavy insurance upon your life,
And cut your throat with a butcher knife,
It's easier done that way.

OAK CREEK, ARIZONA, 1910

The "setfasts" in the fifth verse are sore places on a horse's back, usually saddle sores. This song also is called "The Horse Wrangler." In G. Malcolm Laws' Native American Balladry, *it is classified as B27.*

"THE BACHELOR'S SONG"

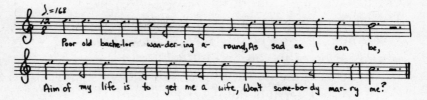

Poor old bachelor wandering around,
As sad as I can be,
Aim of my life is to get me a wife,
Won't somebody marry me?

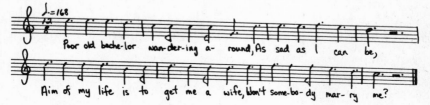

When I was a boy and my heart full of joy,
I courted the girls too free,
But now the gray hairs and the bachelor's cares
Are tellin' their tales on me.

I courted the widows, but they said it wouldn't do,
That such a thing never could be,
But the aim of my life is to get me a wife,
Won't somebody marry me?

I traveled Kentucky from the east to the west,
Ohio to the state of Tennessee,
Found not a girl whose lips didn't curl,
At the untempting sight of me.

Poor old bachelor wandering around,
As sad as I can be,
Aim of my life is to get me a wife,
Won't somebody marry me?

BEDFORD COUNTY, TENNESSEE, 1890

*In a similar song of that period called "Poor Old Maids," a group
of women complained, "We have houses and some land, / All we
want is a handsome man, / Something must be done / For us poor
old maids."*

"THE FIT COMES ON ME NOW"

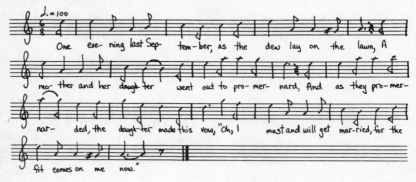

One evening last September, as the dew lay on the lawn,
A mother and her daughter went out to promernard,
And as they promernarded, the daughter made this vow,
"Oh, I must and will get married, for the fit comes on me
     now."

"No daughter, dearest daughter, please hold your silly
     tongue,
You talk of getting married when you know you are too
     young."
"I am sixteen tomorrow, Ma, and that you must allow,
Oh, I must and will get married, for the fit comes
     on me now."

"And daughter, dearest daughter, where will you
     find your man?"

"Oh, never fear, dear Mother, for there is the
  miller John.
He promised for to marry me a year or more ago.
Oh, I must and will get married, for the fit comes
  on me so."

"And what if he should slight you, as has been
  done before?"
"Oh, never fear, dear Mother, in the town there's
  plenty more.
There's the butcher and the baker and the boy that
  drives the plow.
Oh, I must and will get married, for the fit comes
  on me now.

"Cold winter's comin' on, you know, with wind and
  icy weather,
Oh, it's tough to lie alone, you know, when two can
  lie together,
'Tis tough to lie alone, you know, 'tis more than I
  know how,
Oh, I must and will get married, for the fit comes
  on me now."

MARTHA'S VINEYARD, MASSACHUSETTS, 1895

*This song has several versions and many names. These include "I
Must and Will Get Married," "The Fits," "The Humor Is on
Me Now," "Lolly Trudom," and "Lolly Too Dum." A seven-
teenth-century country dance also was called "The Fit Comes on
Me Now."*

"TRILL BIRD"

Trill bird up in the apple tree,
Hum bee over the rose,
Laugh brook ripple in melody,
Sweet little buds unclose.

Wave grass out in the meadow wide,
Leap high grasshopper gay,
Dear flowers never one chalice hide,
Summer will never stay.

Tra la la la, la la la, la la la,
La la la, la la la, la la la la.

BUCKLEY, ILLINOIS, 1895

Street Music

Three or four musicians would stand on the corner and play and sing. In German neighborhoods they would play German music. In Polish neighborhoods they would play Polish music. Then they would pass a hat and people would throw in a coin. Or they would throw a coin from their window. You could hear the music blocks away. It was really nice.

DETROIT, 1910

There were strolling musicians of this kind almost everywhere. In some places they were called "German bands" because such bands were a German tradition. In the Southwest they were called "sere-

naders." Like the others, they played and sang in the streets. But, for a fee, they also would stand under a young woman's window and sing love songs to her.

On Sunday afternoons bands often played in the parks. In some cities and towns one still can see the wooden bandstands where they gave their concerts.

And everywhere organ-grinders, or hurdy-gurdy men, made music with hand organs. Some traveled with a dancing bear or with a monkey that collected the money people gave. "It was a penny a tune," one woman remembered. "And while he played, we jumped rope to the music, and we danced together on the sidewalk."

I Learn the Facts of Life

In those days you usually didn't discuss the facts of life with your parents. Whatever you knew about sex, or thought you knew, you learned from your friends and from experience.

One Christmas I was in this play at the First Christian Church. They needed another little girl, and because I had long curly hair they dressed me up like one. We were rosebuds. So I was backstage with these girls all dressed up the way they were.

167

And while we were waiting to go on, they got curious and come around and made me take my pants off to see how I was built. Then they showed me how they were built.

STOCKTON, CALIFORNIA, 1900

We had this doctor book. It was a great big thick book, and it had all the cures for everything that could ever happen to you. But it also had pictures of all the different parts of the body. So we were not allowed to look at this doctor book. My parents kept it on the shelf in their clothes closet under the quilts.

But on Wednesdays Mother was not at home in the afternoons. That was when the Ladies' Aid met at the church. So Wednesdays after school, my sister and I would look at the doctor book. We took turns. One of us would look, and the other would watch to see if Mother was coming.

LARAMIE, WYOMING, 1910

I was about eight years old and my brother and I, we came home from school, and there was a new baby. They told us they found her out in the evergreens. But with the one before that, they said Doc Christie brought it in his satchel.

NEAR SHANNON CITY, IOWA, 1900

When my brother was born I didn't even realize Mother was going to have a baby. People used to wear so much clothing I guess I never really noticed. But I didn't have any idea where babies came from, and I was fifteen. When I got to be a little older, a friend of the family explained it to me.

BROOKLYN, NEW YORK, 1900

When I first menstruated, I knew what would happen. My mother had told me. So it didn't frighten me at all. When it happened, I wrote her a note. I was going to bed and I wrote, "Mama, I think it has happened." It was easier to tell her that way.

STOCKTON, CALIFORNIA, 1910

When you were a boy, did your father ever talk to you about sex?
No, he never said a word. I learned it in the streets, in the alleys from older kids. We talked about it quite a bit. But we never talked of it at home. And there was nothing in school. If I had a question, I'd go to my friends, not my father.
Why didn't you go to him?
Scared to, I guess. Maybe embarrassed.

TUCSON, ARIZONA, 1910

Keeping Healthy

Every morning I had to take a cold plunge. That was supposed to build up my resistance and keep me from getting sick. I would sit there naked on this little radiator at the foot of the bathtub and watch the cold water running in. Then I'd get all set, jump in, roll around, and get out.

LEXINGTON, VIRGINIA, 1910

Every day I wore a little bag of "asfitidy" around my neck. That was to keep me from catching cold and any other diseases. It just stunk. But everybody wore one, so it didn't matter.

AUGUSTA, GEORGIA, 1895

Asafetida is an evil-smelling gummy resin taken from the root of the Oriental parsnip. In liquid form it was useful for quieting an upset stomach. Many people believed that wearing a cube of asafetida also would ward off disease, but it didn't.

Every night before I went to bed, my mother gave me a tablespoon of whiskey mixed with liver powder. That was to help my liver and to keep my bowels movin'.

ATLANTA, 1905

Every spring and every fall Mother would take a glass tube and blow this dusty yellow sulfur down our throats. That was to protect against everything. Then when sulfur and molasses came in, we took that. That was easier to get down.

INDIANAPOLIS, 1900

The sulfur fought germs. The molasses was a laxative.

HOME REMEDIES

Except in the larger cities, there were very few dentists or doctors. So when people got sick or were injured, usually they depended on "home remedies" to cure them, on medicines and treatments that had been handed down over the years. Only when a problem was really serious would they try to find help. Here are some of the cures they remembered using.

FOR A REGULAR COLD

Mix hot mustard and hot water in a washtub and put both feet in it. This is supposed to draw the cold out through the feet.

SAN FRANCISCO, 1895

FOR A CHEST COLD

Boil half a dozen onions and put them in a chest bag. Tie the bag to your chest and change it twice a day.

DETROIT, 1910

Some researchers say that the onion actually does contain ingredients that are helpful in fighting various infections.

FOR A SORE THROAT

Mix vinegar, lemon juice, a little red pepper, and salt. Then gargle with this.

For a severe sore throat, use an onion poultice. Mix a chopped onion with lard, spread it on a cloth, and wrap it around the throat. Change it once a day.

NEAR LATHROP, CALIFORNIA, 1900

FOR A COUGH

Mix lemon juice, honey, and a little whiskey and take it as needed. Or use lemon juice and sugar. Or heat sugar, butter, vinegar, and horehound until the horehound melts, then use it after it cools. Or peel some onions, bake them with sugar, and pour off the juice and use that.

NEAR LATHROP, CALIFORNIA
NEAR STOCKTON, CALIFORNIA
CAMBRIDGE, MASSACHUSETTS
1895–1905

FOR STOMACHACHE

Fill a tansy bag with dried tansy leaves, heat it in the oven, and place it where the stomach hurts.

DEER ISLE, MAINE, 1900

Tansy leaves come from the tansy weed. A tansy bag is a cloth bag about the size of a hot-water bottle.

FOR UPSET STOMACH

Heat salt crackers in the oven until they are toasty, then pour hot water on them. Eat the crackers for nourishment, and drink the water for heat.

NEAR STOCKTON, CALIFORNIA, 1900

FOR EARACHE

To ease the pain, blow warm smoke from a cigar or a pipe into the sick ear.

KALAMAZOO, MICHIGAN, 1910

FOR BACKACHE AND OTHER ACHES

Mix turpentine, kerosene, and the white of an egg in a jar. Shake it until it foams, then rub it into the ache.

BEDFORD COUNTY, TENNESSEE, 1890

FOR A CUT

Mix equal parts of turpentine and olive oil and apply with a feather. Or use turpentine or kerosene and a little sugar.

NEAR STOCKTON, CALIFORNIA
MILFORD, GEORGIA
1895–1910

One time I cut my toe so bad with a hatchet I had to have it sewed up. My grandfather did it for me. He poured whiskey on it to clean it, then turpentine and sugar to help it heal. Then he just sewed it with a needle and thread and wrapped

173

it up. If you didn't look at what was going on, you didn't suffer too much.

MILFORD, GEORGIA, 1900

DENTISTRY

If you have a toothache, find the cavity and put a peppercorn in it or a piece of cotton with some powdered clove on it. That should stop the pain. If you can't find it, wrap some salt in a rag, heat it in the oven, and hold it where it hurts. If it keeps hurting, pull out the tooth. Loosen it by working it back and forth. Then put a string around it, knot it in place, draw back, and jerk on the string.

GREENE, IOWA, 1895

This was the method for removing a deciduous (baby) tooth. If a permanent tooth had to come out and there was no dentist, you would go to a blacksmith or to a neighbor who pulled teeth.

He'd just sit you down and you'd hug your arms around a stump. And he'd take his pocketknife and clean it in hot water and cut into the gum all the way around the tooth. Then he'd put a pair of forceps on it and pull it out. It didn't make no difference how much pain you suffered. He'd just go ahead and do it. You'd bleed like a hog, and they'd have to carry you home. But you'd get over it.

CARROLL COUNTY, GEORGIA, 1900

In small towns a traveling dentist might come through on the train once a month. He'd have his equipment in a suitcase, and he'd set up shop for a day or two in a room he rented.
What people remember clearly about going to the dentist in those years was the drill he used. To make it go around he pedaled it with his foot. "It went so slow," one man recalled, "and it took

so long, and with nothin' to stop the pain, Lord, I tell ya it was awful."

DOCTORING

When I was sick I would go to the medicine man, and some way he would find the cause. Like the chicken hawk cast a spell. Or the owl would be the reason or the rattlesnake or the horned toad or the wind or some evil spirit. Out of these and others he would find one. Then he would tell me to take a certain herb. Or to break a spell he would sing a special song or do a certain dance, or somebody else in the tribe would do that.

Would this help?

Almost always.

PAPAGO INDIAN VILLAGE NEAR TUCSON, ARIZONA, 1910

In sickness, we called on Aunt Mariah. We didn't have a doctor, but she knew quite a bit. In her satchel she had camphor and quinine and asafetida and different herbs and powders and salves she made up, and the leaves for peppermint tea and catnip tea and other teas. And she would use poultices and hot packs and always a physic [laxative]. No matter what was wrong, they always thought you should have a physic to clean out your system.

BUNKERVILLE, NEVADA, 1910

If Mother couldn't cure us, she would send somebody for the doctor. He lived six or seven miles away, and he would come with his black bag in a buggy or on horseback.

EDGEFIELD COUNTY, SOUTH CAROLINA, 1895

Doctor Simmons was our doctor. For ordinary things we would take a streetcar and go to his office. But whenever it was necessary he would come to us. One time we were on vacation, maybe two hundred miles from home, and my sister got typhoid fever, and he came up there to care for her.

BROOKLYN, NEW YORK, 1900

If nothing worked, there would be the laying on of hands. This was part of our religion, and it was our last hope. Three elders would come and kneel by the bed and pray for that person. They would anoint him with drops of olive oil and pray that the oil would be helpful. And they would lay their hands on his head and one of them would ask God to have mercy on this person. Then it was between him and God.

MORMON COMMUNITY, ORDERVILLE, UTAH, 1900

Death

In those days most people died at home. If there was an undertaker, he came to the house and prepared the body right there. If there wasn't one, the family did what they could. They dug the grave, and in some cases they made the coffin.

Usually the body was kept in its coffin in the parlor. It was there that people came to pay their last respects. According to custom, at least one person stayed up with the body all night. The next day, or the day after, there was a funeral at the home or in a church. Then the body was placed in its grave.

One Saturday night the cows got out, and the next morning my father and the hired man went down and rounded them up and fixed the fence. Father was almost back to the house when this awful storm came up. A flash of lightning hit him right in the head, and just like that he was gone.

We didn't have a telephone, so Mother run to the next farm, to my Aunt Libby. She run all the way, knowin' Father was dead. "John has been killed," she told them. So Aunt Libby came back with her, and then my grandmother came over and some others. Then soon the undertaker arrived. He went right into Dad's room and started embalming him, and I stuck my head in and watched. But he finally saw me, and he shooed me out.

NEAR GREENE, IOWA, 1890

My father's casket sat right over there against that wall. It stood up high and had a glass cover, but no lid that you could put down. My mother was so upset she kept pounding on the glass with her fists. Everyone was afraid she would break it. But my father, of course, he just lay there.

INDEPENDENCE, MISSOURI, 1904

When my auntie died, the women washed the body and dressed it in her best clothes. And my mommy and my daddy went and bought some planks, and some white cotton, and those little tacks that have gold heads. And they had this man make a coffin and nail the cotton all around the outside and on top.

Then we put the body in, and all of us sit up with her that night. The house was full, and the only light was this candle in a bottle. And we sit there talkin', maybe sleepin' a little.

In the mornin' some of them dug the grave. Then they closed the coffin and nailed it tight and put it in this wagon,

178

and we took her to the church. After that, we took her to the grave.

NEAR CADE, LOUISIANA, 1900

Aunt Susan Hunt was a very tall willowy woman. In her youthful pictures she was beautiful. She was slender like a pole. But as she grew older she got bent. By the time she come to die she was walking halfway over and using two canes. She was so badly bent they couldn't fit her in her casket. So they laid her out and tied her down and strapped her soundly to this plank, and then put her in.

Then somebody at the church says, "Youngsters, you should sit up with her." So we went over to her house, but not one of the others would come in with me. They were all afraid. They kept saying, "What if that strap should break and she sits up?" But she never stirred, not once.

BUNKERVILLE, NEVADA, 1910

My oldest brother and this fella were havin' some kind of a feud, and one morning he shot my brother and killed him. At least we think he did it, but they never caught him. This was about three-quarters of a mile out from the ranch, and when we heard the shots we got right out there, but it was too late.

When we found him one of us stayed with the body and covered it with blankets so the birds wouldn't attack it. Then somebody went to Benson to get a coffin—that was thirty miles—and the rest of us began to dig the grave. But he didn't get back until it was dark. So two of us stayed with the body all night, and we buried him in the morning. There wasn't any priest, so my father said the service.

SAN PEDRO RIVER VALLEY,
SOUTH OF TUCSON, ARIZONA, 1911

The heat in that desert region was so severe that a body had to be buried at once or it would decay.

The day we buried Dad the nicest team of black horses you ever saw come up and turned into our driveway. They were pulling this shiny black hearse, and they were just snappy. When everything was ready, they went first. Then there was this long procession of buggies and wagons.

NEAR GREENE, IOWA, 1890

Crime

I used to hear them talking around the neighborhood about the Black Hands and this and that, but I didn't know what they were talking about. I would go around looking to see who had a black hand. When I got a little older, I walked home from work along Elizabeth Street, and sometimes I would see dead men on the sidewalk. These were the Black Hands, grown men from different gangs in the Mafia. To get power, they would kill one another.

NEW YORK, LOWER EAST SIDE DISTRICT, 1905

In city slums crime was a serious problem. But elsewhere in the country this was not the case. There were few break-ins, few thefts, and very little violence. Yet it is the violence that people remember.

Most of the crime here was done by horse thieves and stuff like that. But one time there was a fella raped a young girl and some of the businessmen went down and got hold of him. I guess he was pretty prominent too. Anyway, they hooded themselves up and went right to his house and got him. Then they hung him up on a telephone pole, down there at Lawrence and Main, just lynched him right downtown where the Globe Clothing Store is. I remember him hangin' there, just a man with his arms and legs danglin', and his neck broke, and his head bent over. He didn't have a trial or anything.

I could name two of the fellas that was in on it because I heard them sayin' they thought they had done the right thing. But they didn't even try to get 'em. They figured he had it comin' and let it go at that.

HELENA, MONTANA, 1900

Bill Robbins lived all alone in a house out by Mountainville. Mostly he dug clams for a livin'. He was a fella that if he drank, he probably would get ugly, you know.

It was in the winter, and there had been quite a bit of snow and sleet. So it was a while before they found his body. When they did it was frozen right to the floor in a pool of blood. Whoever killed him had this double-barreled shotgun and hit him over the head with it. The hammers [on top of the gun] left dents in his head. That's how they knew. But they never could prove anything against anybody.

A fellow up the harbor named George Beck was the coroner. So right after they found Bill Robbins, he went up with a horse sled and got him. He had him all covered up, and he was comin' into town. And some boys come along and they say, "Hey, George, give us a ride."

So George says, "Okay, jump right on."

So they jumped on, and they set down right on the body without knowin' it.

After a while George says, "You boys know who you're settin' on?"

And they say, "No."

And he says, "Why, it's Bill Robbins."

Well, they jumped up, got off, disappeared fast.

STONINGTON, MAINE, 1905

There was a woman here by the name of Emma Ledoux. She and her husband were staying in this hotel. And this particular morning she murdered him and cut him into pieces and packed the pieces in a big trunk. Then she had this fella come to the hotel with his express wagon. So he got the trunk downstairs and loaded it in his wagon and took it to the Southern Pacific depot to ship out of town.

I was selling newspapers there that day, and in the baggage room there was this rotten smell coming from one of the trunks. All the kids went up and smelled it, and it was pretty bad. Finally the police came and opened it up, and here was this gory mess of a fella's body. Well, they captured her, and she went to prison for it.

STOCKTON, CALIFORNIA, 1906

I remember at a fair they showed that trunk. I paid ten cents to see the bloodstains.

STOCKTON, CALIFORNIA, 1908

One night we were sitting around and reading, and somebody read in the paper that Emma Ledoux was applying for

183

a parole. So I said, "Who is Emma Ledoux?" And my father said, "Oh, she murdered a man and put his body in a trunk." That's all he said. But when I went to sleep I had this nightmare about her. I got to screaming, and Mother came in and stayed with me.

STOCKTON, CALIFORNIA, 1910

A Comet and an Eclipse

We saw it every night for almost two weeks. We would sit out in the yard and watch it go by. Its head was just a big blob. But its tail was like an ostrich feather that stretched for miles.

DETROIT, 1910

This woman is describing Halley's comet. Most of the people I visited saw it that year. It was a big event, for that comet is visible from Earth only once about every seventy-five years. It was a spectacular sight. Its head was one hundred thousand miles across, its tail one hundred million miles long.

All of us were workin' in the field, and the sun was shinin' overhead like it always does. Then it got smaller and smaller, got about like the tip of my finger. Then it got dark, and the chickens all went to roost. Oh, it was dark. You couldn't see nothin', and everybody got scared. Nobody had told us what it was. We thought maybe the world was comin' to an end. So we got on our knees and we prayed for a long time. Then the sun come out again. Darn, we was happy.

NEAR ALLISON, SOUTH CAROLINA, 1895

An Earthquake
and a Fire

When the crust of the earth breaks and shifts into a new
position, the break is called a "fault." One fault extends up and
down the coast of California for almost six hundred miles. Early
in the morning of April 18, 1906, this fault shifted again. In just
a minute or two the shock waves reduced thousands of buildings
in San Francisco to rubble. When chimneys crumbled and gas
mains broke, fires started. And when the water pipes into the city

also broke, there was no way to put the fires out, and San Francisco was all but destroyed.

When I went down to help Father get breakfast, why, we looked out the window, and over Mount Diablo—that's two mountains west of here—smoke was rising up. And my father said, "I'll bet my life San Francisco is on fire."

NEAR LATHROP, CALIFORNIA,
ABOUT EIGHTY MILES EAST OF SAN FRANCISCO

When the earthquake hit early that morning—it was 5:14 or thereabouts—at first it felt like a pleasant experience. It was a gentle moving back and forth, and I lay in bed enjoying it. But then suddenly the room heaved like a ship, and the force of the earthquake hurled my bed across the room into a wall. So I jumped up and ran down the hall, but the hall was swaying so badly I was thrown from side to side.

When I got into the street, why, everybody was coming out of their houses. The man across the street, he came out in his red underwear. He had a bunch of horses he used in his express business, and he was yellin', "Whoa! Whoa!" He thought it was his horses that had broken loose and were kickin' the side of the house.

Then a fella came along and he had a megaphone, and he kept hollering through his megaphone, "Don't light any fires in your stove! You'll set your house on fire!"

SAN FRANCISCO, MISSION DISTRICT

About six o'clock my brother put in an appearance. He said, "I've got to get over to my office and see what's happened." So he and I walked downtown, and his office was all right. But the fronts on some of the buildings had fallen into the street. And around the corner there was a little restaurant, and it was on fire.

When we got home we had breakfast, and I got hold of some of my pals and we climbed up on the roof of our apartment house and looked around. There was City Hall lookin' like a bird cage that had been belted all to hell, with the birds gone. And we could see fires starting up here and there in the different valleys, and we just wondered how it was going to be.

NOB HILL DISTRICT

When they had used up what water they had, the men fighting the fires tried pumping water out of the storm sewers. Then they tried pumping it out of San Francisco Bay, but they didn't have enough hose or enough time. As a last resort, they made firebreaks. These are strips of cleared land wide enough to check the spread of a fire. To do this they blew up whole sections of the city.

It was three o'clock [in the morning] when they woke us up. They said, "You've got to get out. We're going to blow your house up." In the distance we could see the fire. Mother made us put on our best clothes. Then we took the canary in its cage, and the cat, and we each carried a blanket, and we left. With everybody else, we started walking down Columbus Avenue. Some people were pushing baby carriages and wheelbarrows with all their things. A lot were crying.

NORTH BEACH DISTRICT

Two Wars

In 1898 the Spanish empire included Cuba, Puerto Rico, the island of Guam, and the Philippine Islands. For three years the Cubans had been fighting for independence, and in the United States there was growing pressure to help them. When the American battleship **Maine** visited Cuba and mysteriously blew up, the clamor to join the fight grew. Soon after, the United States and Spain went to war.

The Spanish-American War probably was the most popular war the United States has ever fought. People saw it as a kind of crusade for democracy. All over the country young men rushed to enlist, and everyplace there were celebrations to send them on their way.

I was only five or six and had never seen a Spaniard, but they were the enemy so I hated them with all my heart. I used to say, "I'm gonna grab 'em. I'm gonna shove 'em up a chimney and set a fire under 'em." And I meant it.

AUGUSTA, GEORGIA

My father gave me this picture of the battleship *Maine.* And over here in the corner you touched a lighted match. And there was this little stream of powder that went up to the *Maine.* And when the spark got up there, the *Maine* blew up.

NEW YORK, UPPER EAST SIDE DISTRICT

We would go down to these great open fields alongside the park that now were filled with pyramid tents one after the other. That's where they would get the boys in shape before they marched them off to Manila. But they'd come out here without any toilet articles or anything. So we would take them tubes of toothpaste and combs and handkerchiefs and things like that. Then we'd talk to them. That was the biggest part of it for us.

SAN FRANCISCO

I had a lot of friends who were older than me. They were sixteen and seventeen, and they were all joining up and going. I guess they just lied about their age. But I wished I could have gone along. The war was something that played a big part in everybody's life. The best I could do was join the Boys' Brigade. [This was a group something like the Boy Scouts.] We had military drills and practiced maneuvers and carried rifles, old ones from the Civil War. But we were just tin soldiers.

SAN FRANCISCO

In ten weeks the fighting was over. An American fleet under Commodore George Dewey steamed into Manila Bay and destroyed the Spanish fleet there. Then the American army put ashore seventeen thousand men in Cuba. A week later the rest of the Spanish fleet was destroyed, and Spain surrendered. Cuba gained its freedom. The United States gained the Philippine Islands, Guam, and Puerto Rico, and all at once became a world power.

When the war ended we all went to the parade for Commodore Dewey. It was on Central Park West. Father had gotten seats for us in the Manufacturers' Association grandstand. And my sister and I had new capes for the occasion. Almost all day there were these bands and flags and these different regiments of soldiers and sailors marching. And Dewey was right up there at the front. He wore a white uniform, and he was standing in some sort of a carriage. It was terrific. In our grandstand everybody got a big white box with chicken and cake in it and, I think, a bottle of Moxie [a soft drink]. Father didn't go to the office at all that day. The war was over.

NEW YORK CITY

And then, in 1914, World War I broke out in Europe.

I had never been to Boston, and my father had to go there on a business trip. So he took me with him. We came up from Maine on the Boston boat, and we stayed at the Bellevue Hotel next to the State House. While he got his business done, he had one of these professional guides show me the city. And we were coming along the street where the newspaper offices were, and they had these bulletins posted outside —"GERMANY ROLLS INTO BELGIUM!" "ENGLAND DECLARES WAR ON GERMANY!" And there was a man with a megaphone shouting to the crowd, "Read all about it!"

Going back on the boat the next evening, we saw a small airplane flying over Boston Harbor, and somebody remarked, "If we get into the war, they'll be flying those to Europe soon."

BOSTON, 1914

I Start to Work

In those days some children started to work when they were seven or eight years old, and some worked sixty hours a week. It was not until the 1930s that most states had laws to prevent this.

These white people had a fan up on the ceilin' to keep them cool. It was made of palmetto leaves, and there was a rope you pulled to make it go around. It was nice. When they ate they had this breeze, and they didn't have any flies hangin' on them. I would sit in this little place and pull the rope and move the fan. But if I didn't go fast enough, if it looked like I was dozin', why—"Hey, Nig, what's the matter with ya!" And I'd start it all over again.

NEAR ABBEVILLE, LOUISIANA, 1900

My father made only four dollars a week and there were six children, so my mother took in work. She would get bundles of unfinished pants from this factory. There would be maybe twenty-five, thirty pants to a bundle. And she would bring them home and finish them, and she would keep my sister and me out of school to help. When she started this, I was eight years old.

All day we would sit in the kitchen and sew. We would turn up the bottoms and sew them, and we would put a lining in the waist and sew that. The next morning she would take the bundle back and get another one. I would go to school maybe once, twice a week.

NEW YORK, LOWER EAST SIDE DISTRICT, 1900

When I was eleven years old, I worked in this livery stable. In the morning, I'd get up at three o'clock and deliver horses to the doctors and the lawyers. Just leave 'em tied to the hitching posts. At eight o'clock I'd go home, get somethin' to eat, and go to school. At three o'clock I'd go back to work. At nine o'clock I was done. Then I would do my schoolwork.

EL PASO, TEXAS, 1901

Starting when I was fourteen, I spent every summer working on farms. I packed my suitcase and took a train and would be gone for three months.

Every morning I got the team ready. Then the farmer would drive a binder through his wheat and cut it and bind it into bundles. And I would follow behind and stack the bundles on end in shocks [so they wouldn't get wet]. When the shocking was over, I'd help with the threshing. And when that was done, the summer was gone.

Most of the other hands were migrant workers. In the wintertime they worked on the docks in New Orleans. In the spring they started moving north with the harvest, working on one farm and then another. They went to all the bars and the brothels, and got drunk, and got into fights, and everything like that. They had some awful foul stories to tell. So I got quite an education.

WESTERN NEBRASKA, 1906–1910

When I was twelve years old my mother came to me, and she said I had to leave school and get a job. We needed the money. So I got a job makin' buttonholes in vests.
What was that like?
It was like nothin'. Just work. Start at seven, work till six, six days a week. I got three cents for every two buttonholes, and I made them by hand. Oh, you had to make an awful lot. The first week I made two hundred and sixty-five, and they gave me four dollars.

PHILADELPHIA, 1903

My first job, I worked as a maid [cleaning woman] in a department store downtown. And the first time they paid me I was so proud. I went home, and I took all those dollar bills and threw them up in the air as high as I could and just watched them drift down.

DETROIT, 1914

The first year I worked in the woods I was fifteen years old. This logging camp was twenty-five, thirty miles from the nearest town.
They had me sawin' down trees with a big crosscut saw, one man on each end. Others would be swampin' out [clearing] roads through the woods or hauling logs down to the river. They'd use horses for that. Then when the

ice was out, they'd drive the logs downstream to a mill.

There was about eighty of us in that camp, and we all slept in log cabins. On each side there'd be bunks and in the middle there'd be a stove and a pile of wood. And they had a cook's room and an eatin' room and that sort of thing.

At night, we'd get together in the eatin' room. And some would play the mouth harp [harmonica] and maybe some would sing or step dance or tell stories. And there'd always be some clown carrying on—like me.

There were a lot of French Canadians workin' with us, and they'd get into a bunch and get to talkin', and I could never understand a word of it. Well, we had a water barrel and dippers. So just in fun, I'd go over and throw a dipper of water on 'em. Well, that would always start a roughhouse.

But you had to do things like that to keep your spirits up. Takin' to the woods that way all winter, you worked hard and you never got to town. That first winter I was up there two months straight. When I was eighteen, I stayed five months and eight days before I came out.

NORTHERN MAINE, 1895–1899

The first ranch I worked on, they run fifteen thousand head of cattle. So that was a very big ranch. At the start they had me helpin' the cook. Then I took care of the fences and the wells and the windmills. [These pumped water for the cattle.] Then I got to punchin' cows. That meant riding the range, keeping track of them, taking care of them if they needed it.

Twice a year we'd round up the whole herd. In May, we'd cut out the newborn calves [separate them from the other cattle] and brand 'em. In October we'd cut out the ones that were ready for market. That would be about a thousand head. Then six or seven of us would drive them to town.

That herd would be maybe two hundred feet across, maybe a half mile long. We'd just follow the road, take a shortcut here and there, race alongside, do a lot of hollerin'. It would take two, three days to get them in.

They had a thirteen-room adobe house on this ranch, and some of us lived there, and some of us lived in the bunk-houses. But a lot of times you'd still be out on the range when it got dark. So you'd spread your saddle blankets and sleep where you were.

I liked that. I was seventeen then, and all I wanted was to be out there in all that open space just riding, riding, riding —and nobody to tell you anything.

WEST OF TUCSON, ARIZONA, 1907–1908

I Fall in Love
and Get Married

I first became interested in a girl when I was about thirteen. She was my sister's friend and was at the house quite a bit. She was very pretty and very sweet. I talked to her a few times, but I never told her how much I liked her.

HULL, QUEBEC, 1911

My Grandfather Gifford built me a beautiful boat. It was a small catboat, and I named it *Jenny*. Jenny was a girl I thought a lot of. She was sort of what you'd call my girl friend.

MARTHA'S VINEYARD, MASSACHUSETTS, 1900

In the next apartment to ours there was this girl I got to know. After a while we got so that we would hold hands. Then one time I got up my courage, and I kissed her.

What was that like?

I was not disappointed. After the first kiss, we kissed again, and then again.

BERKELEY, CALIFORNIA, 1910

I had three sisters and often all of us would have our boy-friends over at night. We would sit in the swings out on the porch, and after a while serenaders would come. They were Mexican men with a flute and a guitar and a violin, and they would stand out on the sidewalk and play for a nickel a tune. They would play *"Sobre las Olas," "La Golondrina,"* and *"La Paloma."* The boys would give them nickels until the nickels ran out.

Then a little later often this old lady would come with a bucket of hot tamales. She would have on a stiff starched skirt and an apron with cross-stitches all around the bottom. And always she would tell us, "Never marry."

We would laugh and say, "Why? Why?"

And she would look at us very seriously and say, "At night husband whippy, whippy, whippy. That is why."

SAN ANTONIO, TEXAS, 1905

He was older than me, much older, but he was a very, very handsome young man. He had blond hair, and he played a violin. He could play any of the stringed instruments. I was thirteen when I met him, and he went with me off and on for nearly four years. Not regular dating. He would just come

200

by whenever he wanted to call. I wouldn't even be expectin' him. And when I was at parties and he was there, I would be with him. Then he moved and went to Nashville and from there to Cincinnati. I don't know if he married first, or if I did.

BEDFORD COUNTY, TENNESSEE, 1893–1897

It was just pourin' down rain, and he was goin' somewhere, and he come up on the porch to get dry. I was in the barn milkin', and when I come back to the house I heard my mother talkin' to him. So I went out there, and Ma told me who it was, and he introduced hisself. Then after it slacked up he started back down the road.

I told my mother, I said, "That's my man!"

She said, "You say that again, I'll whup ya!"

I said, "He's mine!"

She said, "He might be a married man."

I said, "If he is, I'll put a spider in his wife's dumplin's."

Well, after it quit rainin' I went down to this neighbor's house, and I described him up to her.

"That's Buck Moss, all right," she said.

"Is he married?" I said.

"No," she said.

"Well, good," I said. "Then he's mine."

Sure enough, he come back.

CARROLL COUNTY, GEORGIA, 1910

Time Is Passing
Fast Now

When I was young I thought that things would always be the same, that I would live the way my parents lived. But the world is so different.

TUCSON, ARIZONA

My land, we go to the moon now. We get on a plane and we are across the country. We drive a car instead of a buggy. We have electricity and telephones and television. We have all of these gadgets that do what we did for ourselves.

WATERTOWN, MASSACHUSETTS

Where the farm was they put in a cloverleaf and paved everything all around. Then they put through these big power lines. Now it's part of a suburb.

DETROIT

I never dreamed we blacks would have a better time in life. I never dreamed that would come. I thought it would always be hard.
How do you feel about it?
It's nice.

FINCASTLE, VIRGINIA

Of course, it's more progressive than it was. There have been many improvements. But I don't think families are as close as they were when I was young. I think that is lost. Maybe we're travelin' too fast.

EL PASO, TEXAS

My sympathy goes out very much to the young people today. It seems as if they have, oh, more temptations and more adjustments to make. We didn't have so many and we didn't have so many chances to make mistakes.

PATTEN, MAINE

It seems to me that people aren't as honest as they once were. When I was young they trusted one another more. Your word was your bond. That was the saying. I don't see that anymore. These days people are more likely to cheat and to shortchange one another.

EL PASO, TEXAS

Years ago we always left our house unlocked. If we wanted to go someplace, we just went. Now you go around your house and lock everything, and even then you worry whether somebody will get in.

MARTHA'S VINEYARD, MASSACHUSETTS

When I was a girl, the world was at peace. We were at peace with ourselves and with our neighbors and with other countries. Today everybody is against somebody. One of my grandsons will be forty-five next fall. The other will be forty-two. They have never known what it is to live in a peaceful world.

SAN FRANCISCO

Of course, in many ways the world is a good deal the same. The kids still go to school and take algebra and geometry like we did. Some of them still study Caesar's Gallic Wars. And they grow up and get jobs and fall in love. And we still have to eat. And the old people still have to be taken care of—it was a problem then and it's a problem now. Not everything has changed.

WATERTOWN, MASSACHUSETTS

When I was a boy one year felt like ten years. Today ten years go by like one. Time is passing fast now.

GREENE, IOWA

Collecting the Past

If you decide to interview an older person about his younger days, you probably will have a very good time. Such informants usually are warm, gentle people who enjoy talking about their experiences, and the information they provide often is full of surprises. This kind of interviewing is not difficult, but there are approaches it is useful to keep in mind.

Before you begin an interview, make at least a partial list of the topics you want to cover. Then organize them so that in your discussion you will move from one subject to a related subject—from where the informant's mother obtained food, for example, to how she prepared it, to what the meals were like. Then for each topic develop a series of questions. Additional ones will occur to you during the interview, but your list will give you a place to start.

The table of contents in this book suggests a range of topics, and each chapter suggests many questions. When you decide what you intend to ask, put your questions in a notebook and use the notebook as a guide in your interviewing.

How you schedule your interviewing also is important. Do not try to ask all your questions in one session. Instead, arrange to visit your informant for an hour or so once or twice a week until you have covered everything you have in mind. Such a schedule helps him to relax and helps you to improve your interviewing. With several opportunities to prod his memory, you also will obtain more detailed information.

Try to tape-record each interview. To do this you will need an inexpensive cassette recorder with an external microphone. This equipment will provide a word-for-word record of the interview and also preserve the sound and the intonations of the informant's voice. Recording these sessions also will enable you to concentrate on what he or she is saying rather than on taking notes. But before you use a tape recorder, ask permission to do so. If a person is shy about having his or her voice taped, explain that it is a more accurate procedure than taking notes, and not as distracting. Also offer to replay any part of the interview and to erase any passages an informant does not want included.

Before you start your questioning, be sure to identify the interview on the tape. You might say something like this: "This is [your name]. It is Friday, April 25, 19—. Grandpa Clark and I are sitting in his kitchen. We are going to talk about his school days." Then ask the informant to give his or her name and address. Then play all of this back to make sure the recorder is working properly.

In your first questions, concentrate on the informant's background. Find out when and where he or she was born, who the parents were, where they came from, and where the family lived. Then begin exploring each of the topics on your list. To introduce a particular topic, I usually ask a general question. To obtain the details I need, I follow this with a series of specific questions. Here is an example of this approach from one of the interviews I conducted:

"If you got sick, did your mother use home remedies, or did she call a doctor?"

"Well, mostly it was home remedies, if it was anything. We only had a doctor when nothing else worked."

"What kinds of remedies would she use?"

"Oh, almost anything under the sun."

"If you had a sore throat, what would she do? Would she mix up a gargle or something like that?"

"She'd mix vinegar, lemon juice, a little red pepper, and salt."

We talked for a while about this remedy, then about others. Then I asked about his experiences with doctors:

"A while ago you were telling me that the doctor only came to see you when you were really sick. Do you remember any of those visits?"

This question produced a funny story. From other questions, I learned what kind of a person the doctor was and the kind of relationship he had with his patients.

In asking your questions, give the person you are interviewing as much time as he or she needs to answer them. If you want to clarify something, make a note of it and ask about it later, but don't break in and disrupt the informant's train of thought. If the informant strays from the subject, but is telling you something interesting, also use this approach. Wait until he or she is finished, then return to your question.

When you finish your interview, you may be startled to find how much you have learned about your informant and, in the process, how much you have learned about yourself.

Preparing This Book

The authors of this work are the one hundred and fifty-six older people who described for me what it was like to grow up long ago. Almost every word you have read is theirs. My job was collecting what they had to say and turning it into a book.

THE RESEARCH

When I began work on this book, I spent two months reading about the years from 1890 to 1914, the period when the people I interviewed were born and grew up. I read books of government statistics, newspapers and magazines from the period, the Sears, Roebuck and Montgomery Ward catalogs from those years, and history books. My purpose was to know this period well enough so that I could ask sensible questions and truly understand the answers I was given.

The next step was finding good informants. To get a clear sense of what growing up was like in those years, I needed informants who came from many backgrounds and experiences. I also needed people who were good storytellers, who had strong memories of their early years, and who would not be put off by a stranger from the East carrying a tape recorder.

Finding such people actually was less of a problem than I thought it would be. For suggestions, I turned to friends who lived elsewhere and also to folklorists, historians, librarians, and social workers throughout the country. I was offered far more help than I could use. Some people sent me long lists of possible informants with detailed descriptions of their backgrounds and personalities. Others suggested I just come along, and we would find whoever was needed. A number met me at the airport and took me around. Some even fed me dinners and gave me a bed.

I did my first field research in Iowa. I took with me two cassette recorders (in case one broke down), enough tape for about forty hours of interviewing, and a notebook full of questions. When my plane arrived in Cedar Rapids, I rented a car and drove to Iowa City. An artist there had arranged for me to interview a pleasant, talkative man named Charles Drollinger. Mr. Drollinger had grown up on farms in southwestern Iowa in the 1890s. We spent the afternoon sitting in his living room talking about those days, and about the fiddle music he had learned to play then, and the songs he remembered and still could sing.

When we finished, I drove north to a small farming community called Greene. A friend of mine had relatives there, and they had agreed to introduce me to half a dozen older people they knew. During the next two days I talked with Clara Weiss and Louis Nettleton, who still lived on the farms where they were born, and Emmett Hanley, who was the oldest man in town, and Edna Wegand and Nelle and Roy Pooley. Then I went down to Independence, Missouri, where an author and her husband had arranged six more interviews for me.

When I got home I prepared a transcript of each interview. This was a word-for-word account of what each informant had said. Then I made notes on what I had learned and marked various passages in the transcripts that I thought I might be able to use later. I also went through the questions I had asked. I dropped some that weren't working and added others that I hoped would elicit more information relating to relatives, cures, and parties. I also listened closely to the tapes to gauge how I was handling the interviews. I found that I had talked too much.

After this field trip there were eight more to other parts of the country, but the pattern for each was the same. I would spend a week or two in a particular area, conduct interviews in three or four communities, return home, work with the material I had collected, and then go out into the field again.

I interviewed many informants in their homes. In other cases we would arrange to meet somewhere, usually at a recreation center for older people, or at a museum or somebody's office. If it was a nice day, sometimes we'd find a park and sit on a bench in the sun and talk. Usually we talked for two or three hours, or until the informant got tired (or I did). Almost always we enjoyed ourselves. Often it had been a long time since anybody had asked about those early years, and there were pleasant memories to savor.

When I transcribed my last interview, I had over fifteen hundred single-spaced pages of information, or five to six million words. The task then was to select from all this the most useful material for this book.

At that point I had a list of about two hundred topics on which I had been collecting information—such things as food, games, parties, holidays, courtship, and cures. First I brought together all the information in the transcripts on each topic—all the references, for example, to going to school or celebrating the Fourth of July or having a tooth pulled. Then for each topic I asked myself this question: "Out of all these references, which ones, grouped together, best describe how things were?" When I had answered that question two hundred times, I had the material I needed to create a book out of what I had collected.

I began this project in April, 1975. I finished it in January, 1978.

THE INFORMANTS

When they were growing up, fifty-three percent of the informants lived on farms or in small towns, and forty-seven percent lived in or around cities. Forty percent were poor. Sixty percent were middle class or well-to-do. Twenty-eight percent were born in other countries or had parents who were; most of these persons came from Ireland, England, Germany, Poland, Italy, Norway, Sweden, Mexico, and Canada. Eighty-six percent of the informants were white. Fourteen percent were black, native American, Mexican American, or Oriental. Ninety-five percent were Protestant or Roman Catholic.

Statistically, the informants seem to be representative of the

young people who were growing up throughout the United States
between 1890 and 1914. Their names are listed below:

Lucy Ackerly
Pearl Andrews
William Ashton
Ruth Austin
Grace Baird
Essie Beck
Robert Belgarde
Mary Lou Bell
Arthur Belser
Robert Benjamin
Theodosia Benjamin
Norman Benson
Minnie Berkemeier
James Bevan
Ann and Edwin Boyes
Charles Brady
Juanita Brook
Royal Brougham
Magdalen Brown
Janie Cain
Sidney Card
Edna Carmer
Amparo Carrillo
Gladys Carroll
George Champion
Paul Chavez
Ethlyn Christiansen
Mrs. Luke Covalt
Elizabeth and Laurence Criley
Henry Crowder
Beppie Culin
Joseph Cumming

Clifford Cunningham
Amy Curtis
Etta Dakin
Guard Darrah
Corda DeBorde
Ivah Deering
Maud Dilliard
Joanna Dinkfelt
Robert Dorner
Charles Drollinger
Joanna Eckstein
Gwendolyn Edwards
Ollie Ellis
Mary Eyre
Alice Ferriel
Anna Fitzpatrick
Nora Fleming
Leila Flynt
Louis Fraass
Chepa Franco
Ignatia Galliani
Donat Gauthier
Opel M. Gauvitz
Ettore di Giantomasso
James Gilliam
Dale Girdner
Walter Goldberg
Elen Grist
Ethel Grubb
Emmett Hanley
Ardis Haukenberry
Ida Hewitt

Margaret Hibbard
Elizabeth Holder
Homer Holmgren
Mildred and E. Gale
   Huntington
Ruby Irwin
Cammie Johnston
Lillian Jones
Winifred Jones
Mary Kaestead
Emelyn Kent
Emma King
Edwin Knowlton
Soon Kai Lai
Helen Lane
Meredith Langstaff
Rupert Latture
Maria Laurence
John Letcher
Oscar Lewis
Juan Machuca
Arthur Maitre
Donald Marsh
Dorothy Marsh
Edward Marshall
Sarah Martin
Anna May McCurdy
Goldie McLuster
Heeber Meeks
Hallett Mengel
Ruth Meurer
Constance Miller
Gertrude Mills
Eleanor Minor
Grace Minor
Carl Moe

Ray Monnier
Avery Morton
Maude Moss
Stanley Nelson
Louis Nettleton
Tom O'Brien
Riccardo Pacheco
Hunter Painter
Ada Palmer
Sarah Parker
Louis Paul
Eileen Pike
Mary Pister
William Pistor
Edward Polhemus
Emily Poole
Nelle and Roy Pooley
Edward Pullen
Elizabeth Rich
Russell Robie
Ethel Robinson
Daniel Saenz
Avelino Salazar
Val Schaff
Henry Schubart
Elizabeth Schuman
Maude Sexton
Henry Shope
Fred Solari
Ben Soza
Esther Spaulding
Charlotte Spence
Mildred Stafrin
John Stinson
Roxie Sumlin
Lee Sweeney

Marguerite Thomas
Thomas Tilton
Minnie Toscano
William Tyler
Hulda Ulrich
Lew Way
Edna Wegand
Clara Weiss

Alice Westfeldt
Rex Whitton
Joseph Wichowski
Elizabeth and Avon Willett
Mary Williams
Walter Winiarski
Marjorie Wintringer
Catherine Woodward

WHERE THE INFORMANTS GREW UP

The place name includes the surrounding area.

Arizona: Oak Creek, Prescott, San Pedro River Valley, Tucson.

Arkansas: Fort Smith.

California: Berkeley, Chico, Lathrop, Los Angeles, Marysville, Sacramento, San Francisco, San Jose, Sebastopol, Sierra Madre, Stockton.

Canada: Manitoba—Killarney; Ontario—Gault, Ottawa; Quebec—Hull.

Colorado: Como, Denver, Georgetown, Golden, Trinidad.

Georgia: Albany, Atlanta, Augusta, Banks County, Carroll County, Dayton County, Franklin County, Putnam County.

Illinois: Buckley, Waukegan.

Indiana: Indianapolis.

Iowa: Clarksville, Greene, Shannon City.

Louisiana: Abbeville, Cade, Lafayette Parish, New Orleans, Scott.

Maine: Bangor, Deer Isle, Hersey, Indian Island, Isle au Haut, Mount Chase, Patten, Stonington.

Massachusetts: Boston, Cambridge, Martha's Vineyard.

Michigan: Detroit, Hamtramck, Kalamazoo, Marine City, Onaway.

Missouri: Independence, Jackson County, Osage County, St. Louis.

Montana: Boulder, Cascade County, Helena, Marysville.

Nebraska: Bethany, Lincoln, Omaha.

Nevada: Bunkerville.

New Jersey: Newark, Trenton.

New York: Hawthorne; New York City—Brooklyn, Manhattan; Rochester.

North Carolina: Mars Hill, Swansboro.

Oklahoma: Woodward County.

Oregon: Dallas, Salem.

Pennsylvania: Philadelphia, Tacony (now part of Philadelphia).

South Carolina: Allison, Charleston, Edgefield County, Hampton County.

Tennessee: Bedford County, Bristol.

Texas: Brownsville, Edgewood, El Paso, San Antonio, Uvalde, Weimar.

Utah: Bear River City, Orderville.

Vermont: West Newbury.

Virginia: Buena Vista, Fincastle, Lexington, Lynchburg, Rockbridge County.

Washington: Ballard, Bellingham, Florence, Seattle.

Wyoming: Laramie.

WHERE THE INTERVIEWS TOOK PLACE

Arizona: Prescott, Tucson.

California: San Francisco, Stockton.

Colorado: Como, Denver, Golden, Lakewood.

Georgia: Atlanta, Augusta.

Iowa: Clarksville, Greene, Iowa City.

Louisiana: Lafayette, New Orleans.

Maine: Bangor, Deer Isle, Indian Island, Orono, Patten, Stonington.

Massachusetts: Martha's Vineyard, Watertown.

Michigan: Detroit, Grosse Pointe Farms, Hamtramck, Royal Oak.

Missouri: Independence, Walker (by mail).

Montana: Helena.

New Jersey: Princeton.

New York: Hawthorne; New York City—Brooklyn, Manhattan.

Oregon: Dallas, Salem.

Pennsylvania: Philadelphia.

Texas: El Paso, San Antonio.
Utah: Salt Lake City.
Virginia: Buena Vista, Fincastle, Lexington.
Washington: Ballard, Marysville, Seattle.

OTHERS WHO HELPED

These persons suggested informants, provided advice, or helped in other ways with my field research:

Arizona: Lettie B. Cale, Arizona Department of Education; Keith Cunningham, Northern Arizona University; Bernard L. Fontana, Arizona State Museum; Vincent J. Doyle, LEAP Community Service Center, Phoenix; Marion Lupo, Pima Council on Aging, Tucson; Ann E. and William L. Roberts; C. L. Sonnichsen, Arizona Historical Society.

California: David Belch, Stephanie Row, Joe Sugg, San Francisco Public Library; Elizabeth Bruenn, Self-Help for the Elderly, San Francisco; Thomas W. Chinn, Chinese Historical Society of America; David Cross, Retired Senior Citizen Volunteer Service, San Francisco; L. Thomas Frye, The Oakland Museum; Raymond J. Hillman, San Joaquin Pioneer and Historical Society, Stockton; J. Roger Jobson, Society of California Pioneers; Sue Lesca, Italian Welfare Agency, San Francisco; Beatrice Schiffman, National Council on the Aging, San Francisco; M. K. Swingle, California Historical Society; R. Coke Wood, Conference of California Historical Societies.

Colorado: M. L. Anderson, R. X. Redmond, National Council on the Aging, Denver; Carmelita Bacca, Little Flower Community Center, Denver; Barbara L. Curtis; Roger P. Doherty, Denver Commission on the Aging.

Georgia: Jean Bartle, Lillie Dabney, Atlanta Area Agency on Aging; Janice P. Biggers, Historic Columbus Foundation, Columbus; Dorothy Blake, Atlanta Public Schools; Talmadge Fowler, National Council on the Aging, Atlanta; Franklin M. Garrett, Atlanta Historical Society; Sammie Lackey, Augusta–Richmond County Public Library; Barbara Home Stewart, J. B. Lippincott Company.

Iowa: Arthur Rosenbaum, University of Iowa; Mr. and Mrs. Vernon Rottler, Greene.

Kentucky: Lynnwood Montell, Western Kentucky University.

Louisiana: Helen Averitt, Lafayette; Francis A. de Caro, Louisiana State University; Mrs. Doremus Dorsey, Lafayette; Patricia and Milton Rickels, University of Southwestern Louisiana; Bernice Zibilich, New Orleans Public Library.

Maine: Dick Alban, Penobscot Heritage Museum of Living History, Bangor; Lillian Getchell, Lumbering Museum, Patten; Clayton Gross, Stonington; Edward D. Ives, University of Maine at Orono.

Massachusetts: Polly Burroughs, Martha's Vineyard; Mildred and E. Gale Huntington, Martha's Vineyard.

Michigan: Joanne Bock, Southeast Michigan Regional Ethnic Heritage Studies Center, Detroit; Freida Gorrecht, Citizens for Better Care, Detroit; John A. Gutowski, Pat Pilling, Wayne State University; Beatrice Jobagy, Detroit Historical Museum; Dorothy Walker, Dave Miller Retirement Center, United Automobile Workers of America, Detroit.

Missouri: Alberta and Edwin Constant, Independence.

Montana: Grace M. Carney, Bozeman; Leslie C. Drew, Museum of the Rockies, Bozeman; Joan A. Duncan, Rocky Mountain Development Council, Helena; Harriet C. Meloy, Montana Historical Society.

New Jersey: Elric C. Endersby, Princeton History Project.

New Mexico: Suzanne de Borheygi, Museum of Albuquerque.

New York: Ruth Antoniades, Sheila Chabrow, Amalgamated Clothing Workers of America; James Hurley, Long Island Historical Society; William Lamble, Edith Moltz, Ed Pulik, American Association of Retired Persons.

Oregon: David Duniway, Salem; Edward Kemp, University of Oregon; Evelyn Sibley Lampman, West Linn; William C. McGraw, Lake Oswego.

Pennsylvania: Carolyn Field, Free Library of Philadelphia; Miriam Sealfon, J. B. Lippincott Company.

Texas: Richard Baughman, University of Texas at Austin; Joe B. Frantz, Texas State Historical Association; Frederico Medina, Project Bravo, El Paso; Dorothy O'Neil, Senior Commission Service, San Antonio; Deolece Parmelee, Texas Historical Commission; Rupert N. Richardson, Hardin–Simmons University; John O. West, University of Texas at El Paso.

Utah: Jan H. Brunvand, University of Utah; Austin E. Fife, Utah State University; Craig Fuller, Jay M. Hammond, Utah Division of State History.

Virginia: Paxton Davis, Fincastle; Chester B. Goolrick, Katie Letcher Lyle, Lexington.

Washington: Bettye J. Gill, National Council on the Aging, Seattle; Elizabeth S. Gustison, Seattle Museum of History and Industry.

The following persons suggested contacts and/or informants in several states: Rebecca Eckstein, National Council on the Aging; Kenneth S. Goldstein, University of Pennsylvania; Joseph L. Hickerson, Folksong Section, Library of Congress; Elinor Lander Horwitz, Chevy Chase, Maryland; Emilie Jacobson, Marilyn E. Marlow, Curtis Brown, Ltd.

The following helped with other aspects of the research: Barbara Carmer Schwartz; Peter H. Schwartz; and librarians at the Bangor, Maine, Public Library; the Princeton, New Jersey, Public Library; Princeton University; and the University of Maine at Orono.

Bibliography

Blum, John M., et al. *The National Experience*, vol. 2. 3d ed. New York: Harcourt Brace Jovanovich, 1973.

Boorstin, Daniel J. *The Americans: The Democratic Experience*. New York: Random House, 1973.

Botkin, Benjamin A. *The American Play-Party Song*. Lincoln, Neb.: University of Nebraska Press, 1937.

————. "The Play Party in Oklahoma." Texas Folklore Society Publication 7 (1928).

Botkin, Benjamin A., ed. *A Treasury of American Folklore*. New York: Crown Publishers, 1944.

Brown, Marcia. *Stone Soup*. New York: Charles Scribner's Sons, 1947.

Coffin, Tristram P., and Cohen, Hennig, eds. *Folklore: From the Working Folk of America*. New York: Doubleday & Co., 1974.

Consumer Price Index Detailed Report. Washington, D.C.: U.S. Bureau of Labor Statistics, 1977.

Cutler, John L. *Gilbert Patten and His Frank Merriwell Saga*. University of Maine Studies, 2d series, vol. 36, no. 31. Orono, Maine: University of Maine, 1934.

Dorson, Richard M., ed. *Buying the Wind: Regional Folklore in the United States*. Chicago: University of Chicago Press, 1964. Includes an excellent introduction to collecting oral folklore.

Fisher, Margery. *Who's Who in Children's Books*. New York: Holt, Rinehart & Winston, 1975.

Haviland, Virginia. *Children's Literature, a Guide to Reference Sources*. Washington, D.C.: Library of Congress, 1966.

Historical Statistics of the United States from Colonial Times to 1970. Washington, D.C.: U.S. Bureau of the Census, 1975.

Hofstadter, Richard. *The Age of Reform: From Bryan to F.D.R.* New York: Alfred A. Knopf, 1955.

Howe, Irving. *World of Our Fathers.* New York: Harcourt Brace Jovanovich, 1976.

Huntington, E. Gale. "Folksongs from Martha's Vineyard." *Northeast Folklore* 8 (1966):1–88.

Ives, Edward D. "A Manual for Field Workers." *Northeast Folklore* 15 (1974): 3–76. An introduction to collecting folklore and oral history.

Laws, G. Malcolm, Jr. *Native American Balladry,* categories A–I. Philadelphia: American Folklore Society, 1964.

————. *American Balladry from British Broadsides,* categories J–Q. Philadelphia: American Folklore Society, 1957.

Leach, Maria, ed. *Standard Dictionary of Folklore, Mythology, and Legend.* 2d ed. New York: Funk & Wagnalls, 1972.

Lord, Walter. *The Good Years: From 1900 to the First World War.* New York: Harper & Brothers, 1960.

May, Henry F. *The End of American Innocence: A Study of the First Years of Our Own Time, 1912–1917.* New York: Alfred A. Knopf, 1959.

Meigs, Cornelia, et al. *A Critical History of Children's Literature.* Rev. ed. New York: Macmillan Co., 1969.

Morison, Samuel E., et al. *The Growth of the American Republic,* vol. 2. 6th ed. New York: Oxford University Press, 1969.

Newell, William W. *Games and Songs of American Children.* 2d ed. 1903. Reprint. New York: Dover Publications, 1963.

Randolph, Vance. "The Ozark Play-Party." *Journal of American Folklore* 42 (1929):201–32.

Rock, Emma. *Tableaux, Charades, and Pantomimes: Adapted Alike to Parlor Entertainment, School, and Church Exhibitions and for Use on the Amateur Stage.* Philadelphia: Penn Publishing Co., 1914.

Sandburg, Carl. *Always the Young Strangers.* New York: Harcourt, Brace & Co., 1953.

Sandburg, Carl, compiler. *The American Songbag.* New York: Harcourt, Brace & World, 1927.

Sears, Roebuck and Co. *1902 Edition of The Sears, Roebuck Catalogue.* Reprint. New York: Bounty Books, 1969.

Spaeth, Sigmund. *A History of Popular Music in America.* New York: Random House, 1948.

Sutherland, Zena, and Arbuthnot, May Hill. *Children and Books.* 5th ed. Glenview, Ill.: Scott, Foresman & Co., 1977.

Tableaux, Charades, and Conundrums. Metropolitan Pamphlet Series XII, no. 4. London and New York: Butterick Publishing Co., 1899.

Thompson, Lovell, ed. *The Youth's Companion.* Boston: Houghton Mifflin Co., 1954. Selections from a century of publication of *The Youth's Companion.*

Thompson, Stith. *Motif-Index of Folk-Literature.* 6 vols. 2d ed. Bloomington, Ind.: Indiana University Press, 1955–1958.

Ziegler, Elsie B., ed. *Folklore: An Annotated Bibliography and Index to Single Editions.* Westwood, Mass.: F. W. Faxon Co., 1973.

Index